Medieval and Renaissance Series
Number 10

MEDIEVAL

AND

RENAISSANCE STUDIES

Proceedings of the Southeastern Institute
of Medieval and Renaissance Studies
Summer 1979

Edited by George Mallary Masters

The University of North Carolina Press
Chapel Hill and London

© 1984 The University of North Carolina Press
All rights reserved
Manufactured in the United States of America
ISBN 0-8078-1620-5
Library of Congress Catalog Card Number 68-54949

To
D. P. and M. P.
whose tireless work and constant attentiveness
contributed to the success of the
Institute's tenth session

Contents

Foreword

The essays included in the present volume were given originally as public lectures during the tenth session of the Southeastern Institute of Medieval and Renaissance Studies held on the campus of The University of North Carolina at Chapel Hill from June 18 to July 27, 1979. They are published here not only as a record of the activities of the Institute but as a tribute to the outstanding quality of the contributions made by the Fellows of the ten summer sessions of the Institute. The proceedings of the tenth session (the last envisioned at present) attest the excellence of scholarship and intellectual stimulation associated with all ten. The closing comments made by Professor David Steinmetz speak eloquently to the point: "The lecture I have given may very well be the last in the history of the Southeastern Institute of Medieval and Renaissance Studies. But even if the Tenth Institute proves to be the last, it will still have served an important function (as did the Institutes before it) by bringing together scholars from diverse disciplines in a common task. . . . The Southeastern Institute, by breaking down the artificial barriers that divide the disciplines from each other, has enabled each separate discipline to fulfill its own unique task more adequately. And for that, we are all grateful."

This volume of papers represents the efforts of numerous people working collectively and individually. The Institute of 1979, funded by the Office of the Chancellor and by the College of Arts and Sciences Endowment of the University of North Carolina at Chapel Hill and aided by grants from the National Endowment for the Humanities, marks the continuation of the Institutes of 1965–

69, 1974–76, and 1978. Special recognition is due the members of the joint Duke–University of North Carolina Institute committee who served in 1977–78 and 1978–79: Professors Frank Tirro (Chairman, 1977–78, Co-Chairman, 1978–79), Frank Borchardt, A. Leigh Deneef, Edward P. Mahoney, Francis Newton, Dale Randall, Bruce Wardropper, and George Williams of Duke University; and Professors Jaroslav Folda, John M. Headley, Aldo Scaglione, Petrus Tax, and Joseph Wittig of The University of North Carolina at Chapel Hill.

I am especially pleased to acknowledge the untiring and inspired work of Mrs. Dora Polachek, who served as the Institute's Administrative Assistant in 1978–79.

Our Senior Fellows were outstanding in every respect; and to them we say again, "Thank you!"

George Mallary Masters
Chairman, 1979 Institute
The University of North Carolina at Chapel Hill

MEDIEVAL
AND
RENAISSANCE STUDIES

I

The Uniqueness of
Florence's Renaissance Experience

Gene Brucker
The University of California at Berkeley

In his classic work *The Civilization of the Renaissance in Italy*, Jacob Burckhardt wrote: "The most elevated political thought and the most varied forms of human development are found united in the history of Florence, which . . . deserves the name of the first modern state in the world."[1]* Burckhardt's view of Florence as the premier city of the Italian Renaissance (to quote him again), "the most important workshop of the Italian, and indeed of the modern European spirit," was not an original perception. That claim had first been made by the Florentines themselves, who extolled the merits of their city, comparing it with Athens, with Rome, with Jerusalem. Florentines never tired of emphasizing the achievements of their fellow-citizens, beginning with Dante and Giotto in the fourteenth century and concluding with such illustrious names as Leonardo da Vinci and Michelangelo, Machiavelli and Guicciardini, in the sixteenth. Panegyrics of their native city flowed from the pens of Florentine writers; for example, Leonardo Bruni, the fifteenth-century humanist who in 1428 delivered a funeral oration in honor of a fallen Florentine soldier, Nanni degli Strozzi. Bruni utilized the occasion to present a eulogy of Florence, modeled upon Pericles' speech in praise of Athens, "the school of Hellas," at the beginning of the Peloponnesian War. Bruni first described Florence's government as a free republic in which large numbers of citizens participated. The form of this government, he argued, contributed significantly to the high level

*This essay also appears in Gene Brucker, *Florence, 1138–1737* (London: Sedgewick & Jackson, 1984).

[3]

of achievement that the Florentines had attained. "It is marvelous to see," he wrote, "how powerful this access to public office, once it is offered to a free people, proves to be in awakening the talents of the citizens. For where men are given the hope of attaining honor in the state, they take courage and raise themselves to a higher plane. . . . Since such hope and opportunity are held out in our commonwealth, we need not be surprised that talent and industry distinguish themselves in the highest degree."[2] Bruni was a classical scholar, a humanist, who believed that the revival of ancient learning was exclusively a Florentine achievement: "Who has called this already wholly lost skill of expression back into light, if not our citizens? Who, if not our republic, has brought to recognition, revived and rescued from ruin, Latin learning, which previously had been abject, prostrate and almost dead? . . . Even the knowledge of Greek letters, which for more than 700 years had fallen into disuse in Italy, has been called forth and brought back by our community. . . . Finally, the humanistic studies, surely the best and most excellent of studies, those most appropriate for the human race, needed in private as well as public life . . . such studies took root in Italy after originating in our city."[3] Now such eulogistic statements were not uniquely Florentine. Every Italian city of any size and reputation—from the great urban centers like Milan and Venice to small communities like Forlì and Pistoia—had its promoters, its eulogists, who wrote in glowing terms about their city: its growth, its military victories, the strength of its walls, the beauty of its churches and public buildings, the holiness of its saints, the great achievements of its poets and artists, its lawyers and statesmen.[4] What distinguished the Florentine contributions to this encomiastic literature was its bulk and the reputation of the authors, whose works reached a much larger audience than did those of writers from other cities.

Florentines were keenly aware of the value of their historians in promoting the city's fame and reputation. Vespasiano da Bisticci, the bookseller who wrote a series of biographies of famous fifteenth-century Italians, noted: "Amongst the other exceptional debts which the city of Florence owed to Messer Leonardo [Bruni] and to Messer Poggio [Bracciolini] may be reckoned the following: from the times of the Roman republic onwards there was not to be found any republic . . . in Italy so famous as was the city of Florence, which had its history written by two authors so illustrious as were Messer Leonardo and Messer Poggio. . . . If the chronicles of the Venetian republic . . . had been written down and not left unrecorded, the renown of Venice would stand higher than it does today. Likewise the affairs of Galeazzo Maria and Filippo Maria [Visconti] . . . would be better known than they are." And Vespasiano concluded his statement with this comment: "Every republic ought to set high value upon its writers."[5]

From this massive literature in praise of Florence and Florentines, there emerge several distinctive themes: the special nature of the city's achievement, her reputation, her superiority over other Italian cities. There was, first, the esthetic dimension, the physical beauty of the city and the surrounding countryside: the churches, palaces, squares, streets, villas. A second theme concerns the great wealth amassed by Florentine merchants, bankers, and industrialists in their business activities that had taken them to the four corners of the known world—from Scandinavia to central Asia—and had inspired the comment by Pope Boniface VIII that "the Florentines are truly the fifth element of the universe." Burckhardt noted this Florentine penchant for statistics, for measuring the city's wealth and her economic vitality in numerical terms. Giovanni Villani devoted three chapters of his fourteenth-century chronicle to a statistical survey of the city, with data on population, food consumption, the production of woolen cloth, the income and expenditures of the commune, even a rare and illuminating reference to the number of students who were enrolled in the city's schools. The political achievements of the Florentines also figure prominently in the civic eulogies dedicated to the city. Leonardo Bruni's praise of the republic has already been mentioned. Not only did Florence share, with Venice, the distinction of preserving her liberty and her republican form of government longer than other Italian city-states, but her citizens contended that, by her efforts alone, republicanism in Italy survived as a viable political force in the Renaissance, in contrast to the despotisms, the tyrannies, that had replaced popular regimes in other cities.[6]

It is in the cultural realm, in literature and the arts, that the Florentine achievement has been most highly valued by her own citizens and by later generations of Italians and foreigners who have made the pilgrimage to the Arno city, to her libraries and archives and, above all, to her churches, palaces, and museums, to gaze in admiration at the works of her great artists. With his *Divine Comedy*, Dante, the exiled Florentine poet, literally created a vernacular language for Italy, making his native Tuscan the model for the whole peninsula. Giovanni Villani made note of the poet's death with this statement: "On account of the virtues and the learning and the valor of this citizen, it is appropriate to commemorate him in our chronicle, for all of his noble works that he has left . . . have contributed to the glory and the reputation of our city."[7] When Dante died in 1321, his most illustrious literary successors, Petrarch and Boccaccio, were still boys in their teens; their contributions to Italian literature would not be made until decades later, in the second half of the century. In addition to their contributions to the development of Tuscan as a literary language, both Petrarch and Boccaccio were classical scholars; their enthusiasm for the learning of antiquity stimulated the revival of the *studia humanitatis* that Bruni had described in his funeral oration for Nanni degli Strozzi. Throughout the fifteenth century, the Greek and Latin classics were the preeminent concern of young Florentine intellectuals, not only professional scholars like Bruni and Coluccio Salutati, but also amateurs like Cosimo de' Medici and his brother Lorenzo, who studied classical literature with Roberto de' Rossi, former pupil of Manuel Chrysoloras, the Greek scholar from Constantinople. Classical literature became, during the fifteenth century, the standard educational fare of young Florentine aristocrats so that, by the end of the century, it was normal for the lawyer Bernardo Machiavelli to send his young son Niccolò (as he reported in his diary) "to Maestro Matteo, a teacher of grammar, to learn to read Donatus," the basic textbook for the study of Latin.[8] If literature, both classical and vernacular, figured very

[6]

prominently in the Florentine claim to cultural distinction, the achievements of her painters, sculptors, goldsmiths, and architects were the most important element in Florence's coronation as queen of the Renaissance. It is the overwhelming visual impact of this artistic heritage that has made such a powerful impression upon the imagination and sensibilities of generations of Europeans. In the eighteenth century, Florence was an obligatory stop on the Grand Tour of young English aristocrats and, later, of their German and Swiss counterparts. In the twentieth century, with the emergence of mass tourism, it is Florence together with Rome that attracts the greatest number of visitors; it is to the churches and museums that they go to catch a glimpse of Ghiberti's *Doors of Paradise*, of Donatello's sculptures in the Bargello and the Museo del Opera dell'Duomo, of Botticelli's *Primavera* and *Birth of Venus* in the Uffizi, and of Michelangelo's *David* in the Accademia.

Florentines were not the most objective analysts of their city and its historical achievement, but neither were their fellow Italians who had their own strong attachments to their native towns and who, particularly if they lived close to Florence, often nourished an intense hatred for their neighbors. Perhaps the most unbiased observers were foreigners from across the Alps, but the evidence from ultramontane visitors is very scanty before 1500. There was general agreement, among Italians and foreigners alike, that Florence was one of the most beautiful cities in Italy and, indeed, in Europe. The Venetian ambassador, Marco Foscari, wrote in 1527: "For an inland city, I do not believe that there exists in Italy, or indeed in the whole of Europe, a more pleasant and delightful region than that in which Florence is located. It is situated in a plain completely surrounded by hills and mountains. . . . These hills are all fertile, well cultivated, and covered with the most beautiful and sumptuous palaces, built at great expense and furnished with all of the delights that can be imagined: gardens, groves, fountains, ponds, baths. . . . Through the heart of the city, passes the Arno, an admirable river, spanned by four bridges. The city has very straight and elegant streets, all paved, so that it is always clean and beautiful."[9] A century later (in 1600) a French visitor, the prince de Rohan, waxed lyrical in his praise of the city:

[7]

"Florence has spread the concept of beauty throughout Italy. . . . It is now at the height of its glory: filled with beautiful squares, beautiful streets, beautiful palaces, beautiful hospitals and beautiful churches; more than any other city in Italy. These features, combined with the freedom that exists here for all types of people, and the creative activities of the inhabitants, have persuaded me to stay here longer than anywhere else."[10]

If the consensus of opinion about the physical city was unanimously favorable, the judgment of the Florentines as a people was just as consistently negative. They were sometimes admired, they were often feared, but they were never loved. They were accused of every vice known to their contemporaries: their greed and avarice, their inconstancy and faithlessness, their pride and arrogance, their peculiar sexual proclivities. Our Venetian witness, Marco Foscari, described them in these terms: "They are weak men by nature and by circumstance; by nature, because their air and sky naturally produce timid men, and by circumstances, because they all engage in commerce and in manual and mechanical occupations, working with their hands in the lowliest activities. The chief men who govern the state go to their silk-manufacturing shops and throwing their cloaks over their shoulders, they squat on their haunches and work in public for all to see. Their sons stay in the shops with their aprons, and they carry sacks full of silk to the masters and do the other tasks of the shop."[11] Factional discord was said to be endemic among the Florentines, as even their own citizens acknowledged. Dante accused them of that disease in the *Divine Comedy*, as did a host of Florentine chroniclers: Dino Compagni, Giovanni and Matteo Villani, Marchionne Stefani. The Florentines saw themselves, in their business and diplomatic relations, as honorable and trustworthy, as never violating their contracts or treaties, but their neighbors viewed them in a different light. Here is a not untypical comment by a citizen of Lucca in the year 1388. He had been sent by his government to Siena, whose inhabitants, he reported, lived in fear of Florentine aggression: "They can recognize the trot of the wolf," he wrote and then warned his own government to be on guard against Florentine treachery: "Everywhere they probe with their heads and their vulpine tails. . . . I beg you to guard your fortresses well, because the accursed Judas, full of evil and avarice, never sleeps!"[12]

Not loved, then, but feared and resented by other Italians; sometimes respected for their wealth and the military power that wealth could buy; sometimes admired for their tenacity and determination in fighting wars. One particularly heroic moment in Florentine military history was the year 1402, when the city was surrounded by the troops of the duke of Milan. The Florentines refused to surrender to their more powerful enemy, who (fortunately for them) died of a fever in the autumn of that year, whereupon his leaderless army melted away and Florence was saved. The Florentines were frequently beaten in battle: by the Sienese at Montaperti in 1266, by the Lucchese at Altopascio in 1326, and by the Milanese in a series of disastrous defeats in the Romagna in the late 1420s. But they rarely lost their wars, which usually ended in a military stalemate and a negotiated peace. The city was not occupied by enemy troops from the beginnings of communal government in the twelfth century until 1530, and only on rare occasions did hostile forces penetrate her frontier defenses to ravage the villages and farms in her dominion. The Florentines were thus remarkably successful in defending themselves against their enemies and, thus, in preserving their liberty.

No one could deny the strong Florentine commitment to self-government, to *libertà*, but critics could and did point out that Florentine liberty has to be understood in a very restricted sense. Despite the claims of Leonardo Bruni that Florence was governed by a substantial part of her citizens, political rights were enjoyed only by a small minority that was recruited for the most part from the wealthiest and most prominent families: the Strozzi, the Capponi, the Albizzi, and the Medici among others. Though a few artisans and petty shopkeepers filled civic offices, most were excluded from politics. This severe limitation on political participation has persuaded some modern historians that Florentine republicanism was essentially a sham and that power in the city was limited to such a small number that, in its essential features, the so-called republic was scarcely distinguishable from the despotisms of Milan or Ferrara.[13] This argument assumes even greater weight after the Medici become the leaders of the Florentine state in 1434. But if only a few Florentines possessed political rights, they were more fortunate than the citizens of the subject towns—Pisa, Pistoia, Arezzo, Volterra, San Gimignano—who were governed by magistrates sent from Florence and who paid heavily, in taxes and in humiliation, for the privilege of being ruled by others. Pisa was conquered by a Florentine army in 1406, but the Pisans were never reconciled to Florentine rule. In 1494 they recovered their freedom, and for fifteen years, they fought desperately to preserve their liberty before finally succumbing to the superior forces of the Florentines. For the Pisans, and for other Tuscans who lived under their domination, the Florentines were conquerors, tyrants, exploiters, not lovers of freedom.

Florentine liberty was thus for the privileged few: freedom from the rule of foreigners for the residents of the city itself, and freedom to participate actively in political life for only a minority of those residents. Yet, with all of these restrictions and limitations, I would argue that the Florentine political experience was unique in Italy and that it was very significant historically. The Arno republic was not the most stable nor the most durable in Italy; that distinction belonged rather to Venice. But like Venice, Florence provided its citizens (and not just a handful but rather hundreds) with the opportunity to gain a political education, to listen to and participate in the lengthy deliberations over problems confronting the state—problems of war and peace, finance and justice—and to be involved in the administration of public affairs, as magistrates in the dominion, as officials in charge of the grain supply, and as members of the supreme executive, the Signoria. No other Italian city, not even Venice, has left so full and rich a record of political deliberation over so long a period of time, from the age of Dante in the early fourteenth century to the age of Savonarola and Machiavelli at the end of the fifteenth. No other city explored so systematically and deeply the basic problems of government: how to create and maintain institutions that will preserve liberty; how to foster a strong civic spirit; how to persuade citizens to make sacrifices for the good of the whole community.[14] It is no accident that the most creative and original political thinker of the Renaissance, Niccolò Machiavelli, was a Florentine and that his ideas were shaped by his experiences as an official of the republic between 1498 and 1512.

The magnitude of Florence's political achievement was not recognized by Italian or European opinion, which tended to emphasize the negative rather than the positive aspects of that experience. Her Tuscan neighbors lived in fear of being conquered or in rage because they had been conquered. Her rivals in other Italian states—Milan, Naples, Venice—were hostile because their political interests often clashed with Florence's. Foreigners from across the Alps were generally contemptuous of this small republic that was too weak to defend itself without allies. When, for example, Machiavelli visited the French court as an ambassador in the early 1500s to appeal for help from King Louis XII to assist Florence in recovering Pisa, he noted bitterly that he was not treated with respect by officials at the French court who viewed him as a kind of poor cousin, whose government needed the king more than he needed it. Machiavelli did get his revenge, in a sense, by writing, in the *Prince*, a devastating critique of French policy in Italy after the first invasion by King Charles VIII in 1494. He showed clearly how the stupidity of that policy led ultimately to the expulsion of the French from the peninsula.[15] But even though he created, in the *Prince*, an enduring image of King Louis XII as an inept fool, he was not able to change French policy or French attitudes toward Florence.

In contrast to contemporary judgments on Florence as a political community, there was general agreement among Italians that the city was the leading center of culture in the peninsula. Not until around 1500, when Rome emerged as the intellectual and artistic capital of Italy, was Florence's primacy challenged; and in the sixteenth century, other cities, like Ferrara and Venice, were competing successfully with the Arno city for this position. Pope Pius II, a native of Siena who was certainly no friend of Florence, wrote this evaluation of the city's intellectual achievement around the year 1460:

In former ages there have been many illustrious Florentines whose names are known even today, but most illustrious of all was Dante Alighieri, whose great poem with its noble description of Heaven, Hell, and Purgatory breathes a wisdom almost divine. . . . Next to him was Francesco Petrarca, whose equal would be hard to find. . . . The third place I should not go wrong in assigning to Giovanni Boccaccio, though he was a little more frivolous and his style was not highly polished. After him comes Coluccio [Salutati], whose prose and verse suited his own age but seem rough to ours. He was Chancellor of Florence, and Galeazzo, duke of Milan, used to say that Coluccio's pen did him more harm than thirty troops of . . . cavalry. . . . He was succeeded in office by Leonardo [Bruni], who was born in Arezzo but had been made a Florentine citizen. He was deeply versed in Greek and Latin and his eloquence was almost Ciceronian. . . . A great many more men might be mentioned by whose abilities the power and prestige of Florence have been increased.[16]

Pope Pius has nothing to say about Florence's achievement in the plastic arts, except to describe the beauty of her churches and palaces. Pius was a humanist, who regarded painters and sculptors as craftsmen—like carpenters and stone masons—and not as creative geniuses whose skills could be compared to those of poets and scholars. There are some scattered hints in the sources of Florentine awareness of the exceptional talents of her artists; for example, in the eulogy given to the architect Arnolfo di Cambio in the year 1300 that is embedded in the legislation granting him a tax exemption. Arnolfo was described as "the most renowned and the most expert in church construction of any other in these parts and . . . through his industry, experience and genius, the Florentine commune . . . hopes to have the most beautiful and the most honorable cathedral in Tuscany."[17]

The painter Giotto was universally recognized by contemporaries as Florence's (and indeed, Italy's) greatest artist of the fourteenth century. His distinction was recognized early by Dante in the *Divine Comedy*:

> credette Cimabue nella pittura
> tener lo campo, ed ora ha Giotto il grido,
> si ché la fama di colui è oscura.

(In painting Cimabue was thought to hold the field and
now Giotto has the cry so that the other's fame is down.)[18]

When Giotto was appointed to the position of governor of the
building works of the Florentine commune in the 1330s, he received this official accolade from his employers: "It is said that in
the whole world no one can be found who is more capable in
these and other things than Master Giotto di Bondone, painter of
Florence. He should be received therefore in his country as a great
master and held dear in the city, and he should have cause for
agreeing to a continued domicile within it. With this many will
profit from his knowledge and learning so that no little beauty will
come to the city."[19] A generation later, Boccaccio wrote about
Giotto in *The Decameron*: "He had a mind of such excellence that
there was nothing given by Nature . . . which he, with style or
pen or brush, could not paint so like, that it seemed not so much
similar but rather the thing itself. . . . It is therefore with justice
that he may be called one of the lights of Florentine glory."[20]

Toward the end of the century, the *novellista* Franco Sacchetti
asked rhetorically: "Who was the greatest painter that we have
had, who other than Giotto?" And that judgment was shared by
an outsider, Benvenuto da Imola, who wrote in his commentary
on the *Divine Comedy* (the year was 1376): "Giotto still holds the
field because no one subtler than he has yet appeared."[21] In addition to artists and professional writers, Giotto's work was known
to Florentines who could admire his frescoes, for example, his
cycle of paintings of the life of St. Francis in Santa Croce. A merchant named Giovanni Morelli, writing in his diary about 1400,
had this instructive observation to make, when describing his sister Mea's hands. They were, he said, "so beautiful that they appeared to have been painted by Giotto."[22]

The fifteenth century, the Quattrocento, was Florence's great
age of the arts, when the giants appeared and when each decade
brought forth a new surge of artistic creativity. It was in that
century that Florence's reputation as an artistic center spread

throughout the peninsula and to other parts of Europe. In his fine book, *Painting and Experience in Fifteenth Century Italy,* Michael Baxandall cites a poem from the Umbrian artist Giovanni Santi, father of Raphael, who wrote that "so many [painters] have been famous in our century, they make any other age seem poor." Giovanni named some twenty-five Italian painters as worthy of distinction, of whom thirteen were Florentine: Fra Angelico, Fra Filippo Lippi, Domenico Veneziano, Masaccio, Andrea del Castagno, Paolo Uccello, Antonio and Piero Pollaiuolo, Leonardo da Vinci, Ghirlandaio, Filippino Lippi, Sandro Botticelli. Giovanni did not bother to mention those Florentine artists who excelled in other fields: Brunelleschi, Ghiberti, Donatello, Leon Battista Alberti, Michelozzo, to name only the most renowned.[23]

Florentine artistic achievement reached its apotheosis in the work of Michelangelo Buonarroti, who was universally regarded by Italian contemporaries as the ultimate master in painting, sculpture, and architecture. Michelangelo's contemporary, Giorgio Vasari, expressed that view in the preface to his biography of Michelangelo:

While the best and most industrious artists were laboring, by the light of Giotto and his followers, to give the world examples of such power as the benignity of their stars and the varied character of their fantasies enabled them to command, and while desirous of imitating the perfection of nature by the excellence of art, they were struggling to attain that high comprehension which many call intelligence, and were universally laboring, for the most part in vain, the ruler of heaven was pleased to turn the eyes of his clemency toward earth, and perceiving the fruitlessness of so many labors, the ardent studies pursued without any result, and the presumptuous self-sufficiency of men, which is farther from truth than darkness from light, he resolved . . . to send to the world a spirit endowed with universality of power in each art, and in every profession, one capable of showing by himself alone what is the perfection of art in the sketch, the outline, the shadows, or the lights, one who could give relief to painting, and with an upright judgment could operate as perfectly in sculpture, nay, who was so highly accomplished in architecture also, that he was able to render our habitations secure and commodious, healthy and cheerful, well proportioned, and enriched with the varied ornaments of art. . . .

And as the supreme ruler perceived that in the execution of all these sublime arts, the Tuscan genius has ever been raised high above all others, the men of that region displaying more zeal in study, and more constancy in labor than any other people in Italy, so did he resolve to confer the privilege of his birth on Florence, as worthy above all other cities to be his homeland, and as justly meriting that the perfections of every art should be exhibited to the world by means of who should be her citizen.[24]

Vasari offers us a variety of explanations for Florence's artistic supremacy. In the passage that I have quoted, he suggests that divine favor was responsible for the gift of Michelangelo to Florence, as an indication of his satisfaction with the achievements of the Florentines (and, more generally, the Tuscans) in the arts. But as the historian of that record of creative achievement that he himself defined as a *rinascità* or "renaissance," Vasari was keenly aware of the value of a tradition of artistic excellence, of standards set by earlier generations of artists, and of standards surpassed by their successors. In his biography of Masaccio, he wrote that the most celebrated painters and sculptors in Florence had all gone on a pilgrimage to the Brancacci chapel to study Masaccio's cycle of frescoes there: "All who have endeavored to learn the art have always gone for instruction to this chapel to grasp the precepts and rules of Masaccio for the proper representation of figures." In another passage in his history, Vasari developed a sociological explanation for Florence's supremacy. That was due, he said, to the fact that "many people were extremely critical, because the air was conducive to freedom of thought and that men were not satisfied with mediocre works . . . [and] that it was necessary to be industrious in order to live, which meant using one's wits and judgment all the time. . . . For Florence did not have a large and fertile countryside, so that men could not live cheaply there. . . . Thirdly was the greed for honor and glory which that air generates in men of every occupation."[25]

How much of this argument can we accept today? Certainly not Vasari's ultimate explanations: divine favor, the quality of the Florentine air, the poverty of the region; but we can use Vasari's descriptive statement as a basis for further analysis: his emphasis on the intense competitiveness that characterized the life of this city and his comment on the Florentine commitment to excellence. If these characteristics were so highly developed in this city, they would certainly help to explain why this community was so creative. The key question is: Was the *quality* of life in Florence significantly different from that in other Italian cities during the Renaissance centuries? If so, did these differences stimulate Florentine achievement in the arts, in literature, in culture?

Let us begin with the most basic dimension of that experience, the economic. Florence was one of a small cluster of very large (by contemporary standards) Italian cities, rich enough to sustain its independence, and rich enough to subsidize a flourishing culture. The Arno city was not the largest or the wealthiest city in Italy: Milan, Venice, Genoa, and Naples were all bigger and richer. What distinguished Florence's economic structure from these other cities was its complex and diversified character. Florence was a center of commerce, industry, and banking; it was the hub of a regional market and of a multitude of highly specialized crafts. Nowhere in Europe was entrepreneurial activity more varied, nowhere was the entrepreneurial spirit more highly developed. The qualities of mind and habit fostered by this atmosphere were: a familiarity with numbers, with measurement; a very sophisticated knowledge of how credit mechanisms could be exploited to make money; an ability to evaluate business opportunities; and a generally pragmatic approach to human problems.[26]

It is in the area of social structure and organization that Florence's distinctiveness becomes more striking. I would argue for the proposition that Florentine society in the Renaissance was the most flexible, the most "open," the most pluralistic of any major Italian city in this period. Florence did have a social hierarchy: an upper stratum of wealthy, prominent, influential families; a middle stratum of petty bourgeoisie, retail merchants, shopkeepers, artisans, craftsmen; and a lower stratum of propertyless laborers, servants, guards, vagrants, criminals. To move up the rungs of this social hierarchy was not easy; it was much more difficult than it has been in modern American society, but it was easier in Florence than it was in Venice or Milan or Genoa or Naples. Florence's

[16]

aristocracy, its ruling elite, was constantly being replenished by new blood from outside and below. Unlike some other Italian cities, Florence did not have a titled nobility with special legal or political privileges before the end of the sixteenth century. Status in Florence did depend in part upon birth, upon being born into a prominent family, but it did not depend solely upon that accident. Other factors such as wealth and personal achievement were involved. Thus, a man like Leonardo Bruni—a poor, unknown, obscure emigré from Arezzo, the son of a grain dealer—could become the chancellor of the Florentine republic, could become one of her wealthiest citizens, and could marry his son to the daughter of the illustrious Castellani family.

The looseness and flexibility of Florentine society is reflected in another context, that of social relationships. This society was "deferential"; those at the top of the hierarchy were treated with respect by their social inferiors, but members from the various social categories did mix with each other. Aristocrats did not keep aloof from the rest of society or isolate themselves in their palaces and villas. Florence was not a socially segregated city with the rich living in one quarter and the poor in their ghettos. Instead, rich, middling, and poor lived together cheek by jowl in the same neighborhood, and within those neighborhoods, social relationships bridged social gaps. Cosimo de' Medici, the founder of his family's political fortune, would have known most if not all of the residents of his neighborhood near the church of San Lorenzo. He had business dealings with the local merchants and artisans; he would sit with them on municipal boards and commissions; he would be godfather to their children. They would address him familiarly by his first name. While recognizing his political power and influence, they would also gain comfort from the fact that they could regard him as their friend, benefactor, protector.[27]

This egalitarian dimension of Florentine social life was reinforced, to some degree, by the political system, which encouraged contact among the various social groups in the city. In the republic's supreme executive, the Signoria, there were always two artisans and shopkeepers, men who worked with their hands and in their shops, among the nine priors who held office for two-month periods and bore the responsibility for the governance of the state. Florentine politics were deliberative, consultative; decisions were taken only after protracted debate in which representatives of every social category above the very lowest took part. The records of deliberations concerning the building of the cathedral in the fourteenth century reveal a broad cross-section of Florentine society: knights, lawyers, physicians, merchants, cloth manufacturers, clerics, goldsmiths, sculptors, carpenters, stone masons— all of whom expressed their views openly and candidly on the architectural and decorative problems of this enterprise.[28] There has survived, from the year 1504, a similar record of consultation concerning the location of Michelangelo's giant statue of David, which had just been completed. A group of some twenty Florentines expressed their opinions on the appropriate setting for the statue. Among the consultants were experts—the painters Leonardo da Vinci and Pietro Perugino; the architect Giuliano da San Gallo—but there were also obscure men such as the fife-player Giovanni Cellini (the father of the goldsmith Benvenuto), the embroiderer Gallieno, a jeweler named Salvestro, a goldsmith named Riccio, a wood carver named Bernardo della Cecca. These men were quite willing, indeed eager, to speak out in the company of famous artists and to a group of prominent citizens, the consuls of the cloth manufacturers' guild, who had convened them to deliberate on this problem.[29]

This involvement of citizens from a broad range of the society in cultural matters was a very significant feature of Florentine experience. Civic patronage of culture, both literary and artistic, was not, of course, a uniquely Florentine phenomenon. The physical character of every Italian city was formed, shaped, by civic concerns, by the community's desire to beautify itself, to create the most attractive *ambiente* possible. These impulses were no stronger in Florence than elsewhere; but, except for a few towns, most notably Venice, they were more distinctly civic and republican than in Milan or Ferrara, where the rule of the *signore*, the despot, created a very different type of cultural patronage.[30] The difference between the cultural achievements of Florence and Genoa has often been noted. Genoa was, during the Renaissance, a cultural desert; its artistic and literary achievements were third-rate at best. Genoa's failure to create a dynamic culture may be explained in part by the weakness of her communal institutions. Medieval and Renaissance Genoa was dominated by great aristocratic families—the Doria, the Spinola, the Fieschi—and these potent clans inhibited the development of a vital civic culture comparable to that of Florence.[31]

To summarize the strands of my argument about Florentine creativity, I have suggested that it was the result of a felicitous combination of historical developments and circumstances, some of which were shared by other Italian cities, but some of which were unique to this city. Florentines had created an *ambiente*, a milieu, in which a man worked hard to excel in his discipline or trade or profession and in which that excellence was recognized and rewarded. Among the ingredients that contributed to this milieu were a productive economy, a pluralistic and flexible social order, a political system that was tailored to the needs and aspirations of that society, and above all, a tradition, a history, of great achievement.[32]

Living in that environment contributed to what may be called the fashioning of a distinctive Florentine personality, the features of which can be perceived in the private records, specifically, in the memoirs and diaries, the *ricordi*, and the correspondence of individual Florentines. It is no accident that there is much more extant information on the private lives of Florentines, from their own hands, than for any other community in Italy or, indeed, in Europe. Florentines apparently were more accustomed to keeping a written record of their experiences than were their contemporaries elsewhere.[33] Petrarch was the first Italian, the first European, to preserve a detailed record of his inner life. His example was followed by humanists Coluccio Salutati, Leonard Bruni, Poggio Bracciolini, Marsilio Ficino, each an avid letter writer who often preserved his correspondence as one way of ensuring that fame would survive his demise. Unfortunately, the Florentine artists of the fifteenth century have left a much skimpier record of their personal and professional experiences. They made their statements with their brushes and chisels and not with their pens.

Most of our knowledge of these men comes from a not always reliable sixteenth-century authority, Giorgio Vasari, and from fragmentary documents concerning commissions or payments for work completed. It is very difficult to learn much about the inner life of the Sienese painter Simone Martini from reading that, in the year 1327, he received 30 lire from the Sienese government for painting 720 gold double lilies at 10 denarii a double lily.[34] We know much more about Florentine businessmen, whose mercantile correspondence frequently contains clues to their private personae. There has survived, too, in the Florentine archives, a rich and largely unexplored collection of private materials written by ordinary Florentine men and women whose personalities are revealed occasionally in remarkably rich detail.[35]

My favorite fifteenth-century Florentine is Giovanni Morelli, 1371–1444. He lived near the Franciscan church of Santa Croce and left a diary, a memoir which, in its openness and candor, its revelation of self, has few parallels in the history of European autobiography before the nineteenth century. The key to Morelli's life was the death of his father when Morelli was only three years old. Though his mother survived her husband, she remarried and he felt abandoned by her. The strongest attachment of his youth was to his sister Mea, who gave him some of the emotional sustenance that he did not receive from his parents, but Mea died early, in childbirth, and young Giovanni had to make his own way in the world. His life seemed to be a series of misfortunes that, in their number and magnitude, remind one of Job in the Old Testament. He fell in love with a Florentine girl from his neighborhood, but her father refused to sanction the marriage. So he married not for love but for social and economic reasons, and his emotional needs remained unfulfilled. He was very happy when a son Alberto was born to him, but that joy turned to intense grief when the boy died at the tender age of nine. In a passage that is almost unbearably painful to read, Morelli describes his feelings of loss and his efforts to recover from his grief. On the first anniversary of the boy's death, Giovanni prays to the Virgin and the saints for solace. After falling asleep, he has a dream in which he sees his dead son who is accompanied by St. Catherine. The boy says that he is in paradise and that his father should not grieve for him nor blame himself for mistreating him. Upon waking, Morelli feels intense relief and his grief subsides. One feels emotionally drained after reading this segment of Morelli's diary, for he has taken us with him on a journey into his psyche.[36]

It cannot be argued that Morelli was unique in his capacity to feel deeply and intensely, but I do suggest that his diary is evidence of a general Florentine trait that is not found commonly elsewhere: to express openly his emotions, his likes and dislikes, his loves and hates, his passions and prejudices. In this realm of inner experience, the Florentines made a distinctive statement, just as they did in their economic and social relations—in their politics, their piety, their poetry, their painting, and their architecture.

NOTES

1. In the Harper Torchbook edition (New York, 1958), 1:95.

2. Hans Baron, *The Crisis of the Early Italian Renaissance*, 2nd edition (Princeton: Princeton University Press, 1966), p. 419.

3. Ibid., pp. 416–17.

4. Daniel Waley, *The Italian City-Republics* (London: Weidenfeld and Nicolson, 1969), pp. 139–63.

5. *The Vespasiano Memoirs*, translated by William George and Emily Waters (London: Routledge, 1926), pp. 356–57.

6. Baron, *Crisis*, chapters 2, 16; Daniel M. Bueno de Mesquita, "Despotism in Italian Politics," in John Hale, John Highfield and Beryl Smalley, editors, *Europe in the Late Middle Ages* (London: Faber and Faber, 1965), pp. 304–13, 330. For pertinent texts in translation, see Renée Neu Watkins, editor, *Humanism and Liberty: Writings on Freedom from Fifteenth-Century Florence* (Columbia, S.C.: University of South Carolina Press, 1978).

7. *Cronica di Giovanni Villani*, edited by F. Dragomanni (Florence: S. Coen, 1844–45), book IX, chapter 136.

8. Bernardo Machiavelli, *Libro di ricordi*, edited by C. Olschki (Florence: Le Monnier, 1954), p. 31.

9. *Relazioni degli ambasciadori veneti al Senato*, edited by E. Alberi, 2nd series, 1:9; translated in Gene Brucker, *Renaissance Italy* (New York: Rinehart, 1958), p. 22.

10. Henri de Rohan, *Voyage du duc de Rohan faict en l'an 1600 en Italie, Allemagne, Pays-Bas Unis, Angleterre, et Escosse* (Amsterdam: Elzevier, 1646), p. 131.

11. *Relazioni degli ambasciadori veneti,* translated in Brucker, *Renaissance Italy,* p. 22.

12. Gene Brucker, *The Civic World of Early Renaissance Florence* (Princeton: Princeton University Press, 1977), p. 122.

13. Philip Jones, "Communes and Despots: The City State in Late-Medieval Italy," *Transactions of the Royal Historical Society,* 5th series, 15 (1965): 71–95.

14. For a recent appraisal, John Pocock, *The Machiavellian Moment* (Princeton: Princeton University Press, 1975).

15. *The Prince,* chapter 3. For Machiavelli's reports on the French attitude toward Florence, see John R. Hale, *Machiavelli and Renaissance Italy* (New York: Collier Books, 1963), pp. 53–57.

16. *Memoirs of a Renaissance Pope: The Commentaries of Pius II,* translated by Florence Gragg, edited by Leona C. Gabel (New York: Putnam, 1959), p. 109.

17. Gene Brucker, *Renaissance Florence* (New York: Wiley, 1969), p. 225.

18. John Larner, *Culture and Society in Italy 1290–1420* (London: Batsford, 1971), pp. 270–71.

19. Ibid., p. 275.

20. Ibid., p. 276.

21. Ibid., p. 277.

22. *Libro di ricordi,* edited by V. Branca (Florence: Le Monnier, 1956), p. 178.

23. *Painting and Experience in Fifteenth Century Italy* (Oxford: Oxford University Press, 1972), pp. 111–14.

24. *Lives of the Most Eminent Painters, Sculptors, and Architects,* translated by Mrs. Jonathan Foster (London, 1855–64), 5: 227–29.

25. Vasari's life of Perugino, cited in Peter Burke, *Culture and Society in Renaissance Italy 1420–1540* (London: Batsford, 1972), p. 4.

26. I have discussed this problem in *Renaissance Florence,* chapter 2. On the mentality of the Florentine merchant, see Christian Bec, *Les marchands écrivains à Florence, 1375–1434* (Paris, La Haye: Mouton, 1967).

27. On the bonds linking Florentines together, see Dale Kent, *The Rise of the Medici* (Oxford: Oxford University Press, 1978), part I.

28. Gene Brucker, *Florentine Politics and Society, 1343–1378* (Princeton: Princeton University Press, 1962), p. 77.

29. Robert Klein and Henri Zerner, *Italian Art, 1500–1600* (Englewood Cliffs, N.J.: Prentice Hall, 1966), pp. 39–44.

30. Larner, *Culture and Society,* chapters 4, 5.

31. Diane Owen Hughes, "Urban Growth and Family Structure in Medieval Genoa," *Past and Present* 66 (1975): 3–28; Jacques Heers, *Gênes au XVe siècle* (Paris: S.E.V.P.E.N., 1961), pp. 509–611.

32. Brucker, *Renaissance Florence,* pp. 213–30.

33. *Two Memoirs of Renaissance Florence: The Diaries of Buonaccorso Pitti and Gregorio Dati*, translated by Julia Martines, edited by Gene Brucker (New York: Harper and Row, 1967), pp. 9–18; Richard Goldthwaite, *Private Wealth in Renaissance Florence* (Princeton: Princeton University Press, 1968), chapter 1; Francis W. Kent, *Household and Lineage in Renaissance Florence* (Princeton: Princeton University Press, 1977).

34. Larner, *Culture and Society*, p. 286.

35. For the personalities of Florentine women, see Iris Origo, *The Merchant of Prato* (London: J. Cape, 1957), part II, chapters 1, 2; Lauro Martines, "A Way of Looking at Women in Renaissance Florence," *Journal of Medieval and Renaissance Studies* 4 (1974): 15–28; Gene Brucker, editor, *The Society of Renaissance Florence* (New York: Harper and Row, 1971), pp. 179–83, 190–201, 206–12, 218–28, 260–61, 270–73.

36. On Morelli, see Gene Brucker, "Giovanni Morelli's Florence," in his edition, *People and Communities in the Western World* (Homewood, Ill.: Dorsey, 1979), 1: 219–55; Richard Trexler, "In Search of Father: The Experiences of Abandonment in the Recollections of Giovanni di Pagolo Morelli," *History of Childhood Quarterly* 3 (1975): 225–51.

II

Sir Gawain and the Green Knight

R. E. Kaske
Cornell University

For Norman E. Eliason

It is startling to recall that when I first began lecturing on *Sir Gawain and the Green Knight*, I could find only one article on it that could be called closely interpretative. A famous remark in a well-known literary history added helpfully that the poem contained "no end of things to exclaim over"—an evaluation that inspired an almost equally famous question on oral examinations: "Exclaim over a few things in *Sir Gawain and the Green Knight*." Today, after brilliant books by Larry Benson and John Burrow and a deluge of useful critical articles, we are likely to find ourselves in the opposite predicament of not being able to cover them all. Even so, I think most scholars would agree that interpretation of the poem has not yet reached a point of diminishing returns; and I would like to outline still another possible interpretation, whose main features, incidentally, took form well before the recent avalanche of critical studies.

Let me begin by suggesting that the governing theme of *Sir Gawain* is a concept that can appear in Middle English either as *lewté* or as its virtual equivalent *trawþe*. One acceptable translation of these terms would be "loyalty" or "faithfulness";[1] and in the context of medieval chivalry this meaning itself inevitably takes on larger implications—something like "faithfulness to all the claims that justly pertain to a Christian knight." (One is perhaps reminded of Vergil's *pietas*.) So considered, the ideal would include for example the knight's obligations to God and Christian morality, to the chivalric code, to his king and his immediate liege-lord, and to mankind at large in their various relations to him.

[24]

This ideal of *lewté* or *trawþe* is emphasized unmistakably at a number of key points in the poem. In the description of the pentangle on Gawain's shield, the pentangle itself is said to signify *trawþe*: "Hit is a syngne þat Salamon set sumquyle / In bytoknyng of *trawþe*, bi tytle þat hit habbez. . . ." (625–26)[2] And in the latter part of the poem, *lewté* or *trawþe* is stressed repeatedly, apparently as the generic virtue that Gawain has been tested for. Shortly after the conclusion of the beheading game at the Green Chapel, the Green Knight sums up the whole adventure by saying that Gawain has been just a bit lacking in *lewté*: "Bot here yow lakked a lyttel, sir, and *lewté* yow wonted." (2366) Gawain replies that he has indeed failed in ". . . larges and *lewté* þat longez to kny3tez." (2381) His next sentence includes a further reference to *vntrawþe*: "Now am I fawty and falce, and ferde haf ben euer / Of trecherye and *vntrawþe*. . . ." (2382–83) The Green Knight's final summarizing praise of Gawain emphasizes his *trauþe*: "And I wol þe as wel, wy3e, bi my faythe, / As any gome vnder God for þy grete *trauþe*." (2469–70) And finally, after Gawain's return to Arthur's court, he accuses himself of *vnleuté* and *vntrawþe*, again with what sounds like an air of final summarizing judgment: "Þe nirt in þe nek he naked hem schewed / Þat he la3t for his *vnleuté* at þe leudes hondes. . . ." (2498–99) And again, "Þis is þe token of *vntrawþe* þat I am tan inne. . . ." (2509)

This emphasis on *lewté* or *trawþe* is obviously supported by Gawain's actions in the two large tests by which he is confronted. In the beheading game, it of course takes the form of *lewté* to his plighted word in the face of what appears to be certain death. In the temptation scenes, the situation is much more complex—involving *lewté* to a number of different obligations, not all of them easily compatible. There is, to begin with, his obligation to the Christian virtue of chastity itself. Then there is at least a twofold obligation to the lord of the castle: first, the simple relation between a guest and his host; and second, the much more complex set of rules brought into being by the game of the exchange of winnings. Finally, there is his obligation to knightly *courtoisie*; hence, I take it, the emphasis on him as a paragon of it, both in the lady's speeches to him in the bedchamber (1226ff., 1248ff.) and in the earlier comments of Bertilak's men when he first arrives at the castle:

> Now schal we semlych se sleȝtez of þewez
> And þe teccheles termes of talkyng noble,
> Wich spede is in speche vnspurd may we lerne,
> Syn we haf fonged þat fyne fader of nurture.
>
> [916–19]

Now the combination of these various claims presents Gawain with an extremely delicate problem in behavior; in particular, how say a distinct "no" to the lady—thus fulfilling his obligations to chastity and to the lord of the castle—and yet not violate courtesy?[3] The dilemma is hit off perfectly by a description of his state of mind on the third day:

> For þat prynces of pris depresed hym so þikke,
> Nurned hym so neȝe þe þred, þat nede hym bihoued
> Oþer lach þer hir luf, oþer lodly refuse.
> He cared for his cortaysye, lest craþayn he were,
> And more for his meschef ȝif he schulde make synne,
> And be traytor to þat tolke þat þat telde aȝt.
>
> [1770–75]

The situation may be further complicated by Gawain's reputation in various other romances as something between a lady's man and a lecher, a trait apparently alluded to here in a number of remarks by the lady (1293ff., 1481ff.) as well as by Gawain's own carefully qualified disclaimer: ". . . I be not *now* he þat ȝe of speken." (1242) In any case, I would propose that what we have in the temptation scenes is not simply the basic Christian drama of whether Gawain will yield to illicit passion but also a complex social situation calling for an unusual degree of tact and wisdom.

If all this is so, what we seem to have arrived at is a pattern in which *lewté* or *trawþe* is to be manifested in the beheading game through courage and in the temptation episodes through wisdom —or, if I can make the suggestion without running a good thing into the ground, in the beheading game by *fortitudo* and in the temptation episodes by *sapientia*. This formula *sapientia et fortitudo*

[26]

(that is, wisdom and courage) is of course a commonplace in medieval thought, as a summary of the heroic ideal; as such, it seems
to me to play an important part not only in *Beowulf* but in a number of other Old English heroic poems.[4] In *Sir Gawain*, the Green
Knight's initial challenge to Arthur's court includes what sounds
like an explicit reference to this heroic ideal: "If any so hardy in þis
hous holdez hymseluen, / Be so bolde in his blod, brayn in hys
hede. . . ." (285–86) That is, if any be so courageous but so lacking in wisdom. Gawain's acceptance of the challenge contains an
equally pointed denial of the two heroic virtues in himself: "I am
þe wakkest, I wot, and of wyt feblest. . . ." (354) And in the latter
part of the poem, Gawain refers three times to the curious pair
"cowardice and covetousness"—all in contexts that seem to imply
a summarizing judgment on his own failing, and two of them in
striking juxtaposition with references to *lewté* and *vntrawþe*:

> Corsed worth *cowarddyse* and *couetyse* boþe!
>
> [2374]

> For care of þy knokke *cowardyse* me taȝt
> To acorde me with *couetyse*, my kynde to forsake,
> Þat is larges and *lewté* þat longez to knyȝtez.
>
> [2379–81]

> Þis is þe laþe and þe losse þat I laȝt haue
> Of *couardise* and *couetyse* þat I haf caȝt þare;
> Þis is þe token of *vntrawþe* þat I am tan inne. . . .
>
> [2507–9]

Cowardice, I suppose, is obvious enough as the opposite of *fortitudo*; the question is, how about covetousness as a possible opposite of *sapientia*?

Very briefly, in Augustine as well as in later medieval theologians, the term *cupiditas*, or "covetousness," has two distinct
meanings: the narrow meaning of "desire for wealth," and the
larger meaning of "desire for more than is necessary in *any* good
of this life."[5] In the latter sense, it is by implication a turning from
the love of God to a love of transitory things, and the basic self-
love that is inherent in all sin; and it is in this sense, of course,

that *cupiditas* is the wrongly directed love opposed to *charitas* or rightly directed love.[6] Again, in medieval thought generally, *sapientia* is the direct antithesis not only of folly or stupidity but also of evil itself, since the rejection of evil is for the Christian the highest wisdom and can be accomplished only with the help of divinely inspired wisdom.[7] Now if, as I have said, "covetousness" is a familiar generic term for evil, and if in Christian terms evil is directly opposed to wisdom, there seems at least some reason for suspecting that Gawain's "covetousness" may be intended as the antithesis of *sapientia* and that the whole expression "cowardice and covetousness" may be a deliberate denial of the heroic ideal from a pointedly Christian perspective.

With this thematic structure in mind, let us now turn to the famous hunting scenes, which alternate with the scenes in Gawain's bedroom. As Henry Savage suggested long ago,[8] Gawain is clearly the "game" being stalked by the lady inside the castle while the beasts are being hunted outside; and it seems equally clear that on the first day the correspondence is enlivened by a reversal of sexes, with the female deer being hunted outside and the male Gawain inside. We may notice in passing that this whole motif of the reversal of sexes is further enriched by an elaborate burlesque of Courtly Love etiquette in the temptation scenes; for example, the highly conventionalized *congié* or formal permission to depart, normally granted by the lady to her lover, here becomes "Þe lady þenn spek of leue, / He granted hir ful sone." (1288–89) With regard to the overall pattern of the hunting scenes, Savage proposed that the character and behavior of the three beasts hunted on the successive days—deer, boar, and fox—are meant to parallel the changing tactics of Gawain on the three days. I would suggest instead that the animals represent emblematically the dangers latent in his situation and that their fates represent the fate which awaits him if he fails. The thirteenth-century encyclopedist Thomas of Cantimpré, for example, moralizes the doe as those who are too slack and cowardly of mind to resist temptation: "[Dammule] illos signant, qui animo segnes et ignavi resistere nolunt dyabolo temptatori; et ideo variis morsibus vitiorum horis omnibus demones in eos debachantur. . . ."[9] The usual characteristics of the boar in medieval encyclopedias are ferocity and what might be called boorishness: "Aper, id est porcus, vel sus silvester a feritate vocatur, ablata scilicet littera quasi asper, ut vult Varro. Unde apud Græcos, agrios, ἄγριος, id est agrestis, ferus dicitur et ferox, omne enim quod ferum est et immite abusive agreste vocamus."[10] We have already noticed that Gawain's test in the bedroom scenes involves the extremely complex feat of not sleeping with the lady, while at the same time not slipping into ungraciousness in his refusal. If this is so, might the slack and cowardly doe stand for those qualities that would make him not resist directly enough, that is, preserve courtesy but fail in chastity? And might the fierce and boorish boar stand for those qualities that would make him resist too directly, that is, preserve chastity but fail in courtesy? And would the fox, with his common reputation for trickery and baseness,[11] then stand for the slight contamination of both wisdom and fortitude (the first by wiliness, the second by a touch of fear) that makes him finally accept the girdle?

Such an interpretation would be supported also by the obvious correspondence between the fate that awaits Gawain under the ax of the green man and the detailed descriptions of the cutting up of the deer and the boar, both of which make prominent mention of the cutting off of the head (1353, 1607). This observation, in turn, leads us to look more closely at the image of *brittening*, that is, "breaking up" or "cutting up," a word frequently used for the dismembering of game animals.[12] The verb *britten* appears four times in the poem, including one occurrence in the cutting up of the deer (1339) and one in the cutting up of the boar (1611). Of the two other occurrences, one is in the lament by the people of Arthur's court when Gawain rides off to keep his appointment with the Green Knight:

> A lowande leder of ledez in londe hym wel semez,
> And so had better haf ben þen *britned* to noȝt,
> Hadet wyth an aluisch mon, for angardez pryde.
>
> [679–81]

I take this as a hint of what the result will be if Gawain, as the "game" to be hunted inside the castle, is, so to speak, "taken";

presumably his fate would then approximate that of the game animals. The other use of the word *britten* is in the opening lines of the poem: "Siþen þe sege and þe assaut watz sesed at Troye, / Þe borȝ *brittened* and brent to brondez and askez. . . ." (1–2) Now Troy is a spectacular example of a city that fell victim not merely to force but to a combination of force and cunning (the wooden horse and all that), as is immediately alluded to in the lines that follow (3–4). Are we to understand, then, that Troy fell through a failure of *sapientia et fortitudo,* and was accordingly *brittened* like the beasts representing Gawain's possible fate?

The thematic importance of Troy in the poem is emphasized by its reoccurrence in the closing lines (2525), as well as by a comparison in which Bertilak's servant tells Gawain that the Green Knight is bigger than either the best four of Arthur's knights or Hector (2100–2). The most prominent connection of Troy with Arthur's court, of course, is the fact that the Britons were held to be descendants of the Trojans by way of Brutus, a legendary descendant of Aeneas, who like him undertook a long, eventful voyage to found a new nation. What emerges, I think, is a pattern in which Arthur's young court, the descendants of the Trojans, are tested in the person of Gawain and, for the time being, survive—as Troy in the end did not. Surely, however, it is also significant that Troy fell because of a woman; that one means of tempting Gawain is a woman; and that at some time in the future, Arthur's court is itself destined to fall through the unfaithfulness of Guinivere.

One common medieval significance of Troy is as an example of pride that was humbled; this tradition, apparently based on the words "Postquam . . . ceciditque superbum Ilium" in the *Aeneid* (III, 1–3), is for example dramatized on the ledge of the proud in Dante's *Purgatorio.*[13] In *Sir Gawain and the Green Knight,* the testing of Arthur's court in the person of Gawain, along with his small partial failure, seems clearly bound up with a potential vulnerability to pride. The Green Knight first challenges the court by asking, "Where is now your *sourquydrye* and your *conquestes* . . . ?" (311) After the completion of the beheading game, he reveals that Morgain la Fée sent him "For to assay þe *surquidré,* ȝif hit soth were / Þat rennes of þe grete renoun of þe Rounde Table." (2457–58) Finally, Gawain remarks ruefully that in future he will look at the green girdle ". . . quen *pryde* schal me pryk for prowes of armes." (2437) Pride—as inordinate love of self, the preference for one's own desires over one's obligations to God and man—would in Augustinian terms be identical with the cupidity, or desire for more than is necessary in earthly goods, that I suggested earlier as the meaning of Gawain's *couetyse;*[14] and both would form a natural antithesis to the *lewté* or *trawþe* that I have proposed as the governing theme of the poem.[15]

So far, I have tried to show that the controlling ideal in *Sir Gawain and the Green Knight* is this virtue of *lewté* or *trawþe*, closely supported by the heroic ideal *sapientia et fortitudo;* and that this pattern of values informs not only the two main actions of the poem but also the hunting scenes, the theme of *brittening*, and the allusions to Troy. Gawain's slight failure in accepting the girdle seems nicely calculated as a minor defect in both of the heroic virtues—a small mistake in judgment as well as a small departure from courage. In a larger way, it is a semicomic acknowledgment of the inevitable imperfection of even this paragon of knighthood, aided and abetted by the tolerant laughter of Arthur's court, with God knows what sly comment on the "Arthur's Court" of the poet's own time and place. With regard to the vexed question of Gawain's two "confessions"—the first to the priest at Bertilak's castle (1876–84), the second to the Green Knight himself after the final confrontation (2369–94)—I suspect that the emphasis often placed on the question about the validity of the first confession is somewhat beside the point.[16] That it is to be regarded as valid seems almost inescapable, in view of the poet's description of the effects of the absolution: "And he asoyled hym surely and sette hym so clene / As domezday schulde haf ben diȝt on þe morn." (1883–84) However that may be, I would suggest that these two passages are employed mainly as a pair of related devices to illuminate Gawain's psychological state before and after the final showdown with the Green Knight. His confession to the priest, while sincere and presumably valid in ordinary Christian terms, does reveal by implication a possibly unconscious chink in his spiritual armor: a basic, almost unavoidable attachment to life itself. His later "confession" to the Green Knight is a rueful lament over this hitherto unsuspected imperfection. The fact that the first confession is to a representative of established Christianity who absolves and the second to a mysterious green apparition who on the whole condones (and who, I will suggest presently, is to be thought of from one perspective as nature itself) would provide its own wry comment on the never quite eradicable presence of natural man, even in so Christian a knight as Gawain. A word should be said also about the obvious fact that both of Gawain's major tests turn out in the end to be games, artificially contrived; the closer one looks, the more the poem is in fact saturated with this "game" atmosphere.[17] The essence of a game is that it exists in a vacuum of sorts, testing highly specific skills by means of its own rules, which have no necessary connection with real life. Just so, I take it, the point of the "game" situation in *Sir Gawain* is to throw the emphasis onto the tests of Gawain *as tests* and so onto his virtue *as virtue*, apart from complicating realities.

Time forbids an inclusive analysis of the many other difficulties that would of course have to be accounted for in an interpretation of this kind. By way of example, however, let us consider two of the most formidable, beginning with the notorious puzzle of the pentangle painted on Gawain's shield (623–65), which is explained by the poet as embracing five groups of five: the five *wyttez* or five senses (640); the five fingers (641); *afyaunce* (trust or faith) in the five wounds of Christ (642); *forsnes* (fortitude) inspired by the five joys of Mary (646); and an apparently miscellaneous group of five virtues:

þe fyft fyue þat I finde þat þe frek vsed
Watz *fraunchyse* and *felaȝschyp* forbe al þyng,
His *clannes* and his *cortaysye* croked were neuer,
And *pité*, þat passez alle poyntez, þyse pure fyue
Were harder happed on þat haþel þen on any oþer.

[651–55]

Though incidental light has been thrown on this curious device in a number of studies,[18] what seem to me its central questions remain unanswered: first, what is the significance of the fifth group of five virtues, for which no exact parallel has ever been found? second and more important, why *these* five fives brought together in one figure? In the wilderness of medieval number symbolism, one thing that stands out consistently about the number five is its connection with the five senses and the material realm in which they operate. Dante, in the *Convivio*, compares the pentangle itself to man completed by reason.[19] Some such meaning seems at least plausible for its use in *Sir Gawain*, with perhaps a hint of its status as a "spherical" number (one that reproduces itself endlessly when squared and so signifies perfection) in the five groups of five that make up the pentangle as a whole. Again, it seems fairly clear that the pentangle somehow gets replaced by the green girdle as Gawain's talisman of protection in the latter part of the poem. But when a poet as good as this one stops his story so abruptly and for so long to introduce a static device (even calling attention to the fact, as he does in line 624 with the remark "þof tary hyt me schulde"), and when the device itself is so complicated and so carefully worked out, I think we are justified in looking for something more.

My own attack on the problem is outlined in Diagram 1. The first two groups of five I take to pertain to natural man, that is, to man simply as man, without the redeeming grace of Christianity. The first group—the five *wyttez* or senses—represent a natural means to knowledge and thus relate to *sapientia*; the second group —the five fingers—represent a natural means to deeds and relate to *fortitudo*. I then consider the third and fourth groups of five as pertaining to specifically Christian man. The third group— *afyaunce*, trust or faith in the five wounds of Christ—I take to relate to Christian *sapientia*, by way of the profound connection between faith and wisdom;[20] the fourth group—*forsnes* or fortitude inspired by the five joys of Mary—seems related obviously enough to Christian *fortitudo*. (In these last two groups, the important concepts for this scheme would of course be not the five wounds and five joys themselves but the faith and fortitude they inspire.) If we understand these first four groups of five as defining Gawain's character and career in a general way, I wonder whether it is not possible to see in the mysterious fifth group an anticipation of the

Diagram 1

	Related to *sapientia*	Related to *fortitudo*
Natural man	5 *wyttez* (senses): means to knowledge	5 *fyngres*: means to deeds
Christian man	*afyaunce* (trust, faith) in 5 wounds of Christ	*forsnes* (fortitude) inspired by 5 joys of Mary

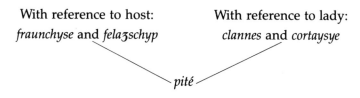

With reference to host: With reference to lady:
fraunchyse and *fela3schyp*   *clannes* and *cortaysye*

pité

virtues he is expected to demonstrate at the castle of Bertilak, with the first two—*fraunchyse* and *fela3schyp*—relating to Bertilak himself, and the next two—*clannes* and *cortaysye*—relating to the lady. Both *fraunchyse* (liberality) and *fela3schyp* (which I take to mean a spirit of brotherhood with one's fellow man) seem integral components of the game of the exchange of winnings; and we have already noticed the prominent role of *clannes* and *cortaysye* (chastity and courtesy) in Gawain's dealings with the lady. The final virtue of the five, *pité*, can be understood either as "piety" or as "pity"; I would read it primarily as "piety" and interpret it as an epitome not only of the preceding four virtues but also of the other groups of five and of everything Gawain is expected to be—that is, as a virtual equivalent of the pervasive *lewté* and *trawþe*.

If this suggestion can be entertained without hilarity, there may just possibly be a further pattern based on it. In the account of the pentangle, the reference to the five joys of Mary is followed by a description of the picture of Mary also painted on Gawain's shield:

[34]

At þis cause þe knyȝt comlyche hade
In þe inore half of his schelde hir ymage depaynted,
Þat quen he blusched þerto his belde neuer payred.

[648–50]

The detail itself is of course a commonplace in Arthurian literature; but as far as I know, the closest parallel to this description in
Sir Gawain occurs in Robert Holkot's tremendously popular commentary on the Book of Wisdom, written during the 1330s:

Scutum nostrum est fides nostra, ad Ephes. 6[:16], "In omnibus sumentes
scutum fidei in quo possitis omnia tela nequissimi ignea extinguere." In
historia Britonum scribitur de Archturo rege, quod in interiori parte scuti
sui imaginem Virginis gloriosæ depictam habuit, quam quotiens in bello
fatigatus aspexit, spem recuperauit & uires. Isto modo nos si in bello uitæ
præsentis triumphare uelimus, infra scutum fidei nostræ imaginem uirgi-
nis cum filio deportemus. . . .[21]

Let us notice particularly here the emphasis on the virtues faith
and hope, both connected with Mary; in *Sir Gawain*, what seem to
be the same ideas are associated with the five wounds of Christ
and the five joys of Mary. Gawain's *afyaunce* in the five wounds
(642) can easily be understood as an allusion to faith. His *forsnes*
and *belde* inspired by the five joys and the picture of Mary (646,
650) can be connected, though perhaps less obviously, with hope,
the militant virtue; to say that whenever he gazed on the Virgin's
picture *his belde neuer payred* ("his boldness never faltered") is,
after all, quite close to saying that his hope never faltered. If this
equation still seems suspect, we may note the explicit connection
between hope and strength, both inspired by Mary, in our passage
from Holkot: ". . . so often as he looked at her . . . he recovered
hope and strength."

Now faith and hope, which I have just suggested are related to
the five wounds and five joys within Gawain's pentangle, are of
course the first two of the Theological Virtues—Faith, Hope, and
Charity—and since the Theological Virtues are the virtues that
perfect man specifically as a Christian, they would fall in the right
place in my earlier scheme, presented in the diagram. The virtues
that perfect man simply as man are the four Cardinal Virtues,

[35]

Prudence, Justice, Temperance, and Fortitude. I wonder, then, whether the poet may not be using the first two fives—the five senses and five fingers, symbolizing *sapientia et fortitudo* in terms of natural man—as a kind of summarizing allusion to the Cardinal Virtues, or, let us say, as covering the same general ground as the Cardinal Virtues.[22] If so, he would then seem to be using *afyaunce* in the five wounds of Christ as a synecdoche for Faith (the first of the Theological Virtues) and relating both of them to Christian wisdom; and in the same way he would seem to be associating *forsnes* and *belde* inspired by the five joys and the picture of Mary with Hope (the second of the Theological Virtues) and relating both of them to Christian fortitude. If this pattern should be at all plausible, the meaning of the mysterious final group of five virtues—liberality, fellowship, chastity, courtesy, and piety or pity—would become obvious: Charity, the last of the three Theological Virtues, seen in those aspects that have a particular relation to the chivalric life, to Gawain's present situation, and to the pentangle as I have interpreted it. On the face of it such an explanation seems possible enough, and it is not difficult to find traditional connections between each of the five individual virtues and charity;[23] the only catch is that I have not yet found them related to charity as a well-defined group (imagine, if you will, the chore of reading through the corpus of medieval pronouncements on charity). I should add, incidentally, that one of my undergraduates a few years ago greeted this whole proposal about the pentangle, complete with diagram, with the brief but heartfelt comment, "What a hell of a way to have to read a poem!" Further questioning made it clear that what he was objecting to was a certain exacting mechanical quality, which may not have escaped the present audience. Whatever one may think about that problem—and there are many attitudes possible—it is at least worth recalling that the present passage seems unabashedly to invite this sort of regimented interpretation through its own preoccupation with a pattern of five carefully explicated fives.

Finally, let us turn to the enigmatic figures of the Green Knight and the two ladies, all of whom would seem to be outstanding candidates for some sort of extraliteral interpretation. To begin with, how about the Green Knight as a figure of Nature? His greenness would be obviously appropriate; his carrying a bob of holly in one hand and an ax in the other (206–8) would hit off nicely the benevolent and the hostile aspects of nature; and there is even a certain aptness in the game he proposes, a demonstration of the proposition "You can't damage me permanently, but I can easily kill you," which, however inadequate it might be as a speech of nature to modern man, must surely have been an accurate summary of the medieval situation. At several points in the hunting scenes, the Green Knight (alias lord of the castle) seems in his joyous frenzy almost to become one with nature (1174–77, 1590–91); and the speech of the servant, warning Gawain not to seek out the Green Knight, describes him in terms that would apply perfectly to nature itself:

> Þer passes non bi þat place so proude in his armes
> Þat he ne dyngez hym to deþe with dynt of his honde;
> For he is a mon methles, and mercy non vses,
> For be hit chorle oþer chaplayn þat bi þe chapel rydes,
> Monk oþer masseprest, oþer any mon elles,
> Hym þynk as queme hym to quelle as quyk go hymseluen.
>
> [2104–9]

With regard to the traditions probably underlying the portrayal of the Green Knight, I agree with Professor Benson that the image itself seems derived primarily from the "green man" and the "wild man" so familiar in medieval folklore, literature, and art.[24] The "green man" is of course intimately connected with nature, through the theme of fertility; he is also closely associated with decapitation and with the cycle of the seasons, both prominent themes in *Sir Gawain*. I would also suggest, however, that the poet has adapted these popular images into a vehicle for a sophisticated and highly philosophical conception of nature—that of Nature as one of the two regents through whom God runs the material universe, somewhat like, say, the Nature who appears in Alain de Lille's *Anticlaudianus* and *De planctu Naturae* or for that

[37]

matter in Chaucer's *Parlement of Foules*. It is in this way, I take it, that the Green Knight can be apparent enemy, deceptive tester, and benign yet righteous judge, all in one.

We come at last to the two ladies, the old one and the young one. Literally, of course, the old one is identified as Morgain la Fée; and at least a plausible motive for her enmity toward Guinivere and Arthur's court (2456ff.) can be found in certain romances of the Vulgate Cycle, where she is forced to leave the court because of a love affair that has been discovered and exposed by Guinivere. But if the Green Knight can be suspected of somehow suggesting Nature, one may reasonably ask whether there may not also be something more to the ladies. Hans Schnyder, in a book in which I can find little to agree with, proposes for them an interpretation I had often wondered about: that together they function as a symbol of Fortune, who is often presented as having two faces, one pleasant, the other unpleasant.[25] Sometimes, indeed, the pleasant face or pleasant side of Fortune is white, while her unpleasant face or side is black[26]—a detail that corresponds rather well to part of the poet's introductory description of the two ladies:

> Bot vnlyke on to loke þo ladyes were,
> For if þe ȝonge watz ȝep, ȝolȝe watz þat oþer;
> Riche red on þat on rayled ayquere,
> Rugh ronkled chekez þat oþer on rolled;
> Kerchofes of þat on, wyth mony cler perlez,
> Hir brest and hir *bryȝt þrote* bare displayed,
> Schon *schyrer þen snawe* þat schedez on hillez;
> Þat oþer wyth a gorger watz gered ouer þe swyre,
> Chymbled ouer hir *blake chyn* with chalkquyte vayles,
> Hir frount folden in sylk, enfoubled ayquere,
> Toreted and treleted with tryflez aboute,
> Þat noȝt watz bare of þat burde bot þe *blake broȝes*,
> Þe tweyne yȝen and þe nase, þe naked lyppez,
> And þose were soure to se and sellyly blered. . . .

[950–63]

In the German romance *Diu Krône*, written in the early thirteenth century by Heinrîch von dem Türlîn, Sir Gawain himself encounters a Lady Fortune who on the right side is "adorned with great richness, both body and clothing," and on the left side appears "old, blind, black, and faded":

> Vrou Sælde und ir kint, daz Heil,
> Die wâren an dem rehten teil
> Geziert von grôzer rîcheit
> Beidiu lîp unde kleit,
> Und was nâch vröuden gar gestalt;
> Zer andern sîte schinen sie alt,
> Blint, swarz unde bleich. . . .[27]

It may also be worth noticing that Morgain la Fée and Lady Fortune are both goddesses and that at least one part of the Green Knight's later description of Morgain would apply about equally well to Fortune:

> Morgne þe goddes
> Þerfore hit is hir name:
> Weldez non so hyȝe hawtesse
> Þat ho ne con make ful tame.
>
> [2452–55]

In the poem, the old woman does indeed send Gawain harsh fortune by way of the Green Knight, while the younger one offers him pleasant fortune. An association of the young woman with the pleasant aspect of Fortune might be favored also by the evident connection between Gawain's "three temptations" at her hand and the famous trinity of evils in I John 2:16, "concupiscentia carnis . . . et concupiscentia oculorum et superbia vitae";[28] in the roughly contemporary poem *Piers Plowman* (B, XI, 12–15) the dreamer is tempted by Fortune herself, who is attended by "*Concupiscencia carnis*," "Coueitise of eiȝes," and "Pride of parfit lyuynge." If this whole identification of the Green Knight and the two ladies in *Sir Gawain* is convincing, Gawain's testers take on overtones of *Natura* and *Fortuna*, the two great regents by whom God

R. E. Kaske

rules the material universe; the test of the Round Table through Gawain takes on cosmic proportions, surpassing even those it acquires by the comparison with Troy; and the result is to show man his limitations as man in the presence of these two great controlling forces.

NOTES

1. *MED*, L.2, p. 734, "leautę n.," especially (b); *NED*, "Lewty," "Lealty[1]," "Troth, *sb. arch.*, I.1," and "Truth, *sb.*, I.1"; and J. A. Burrow, *A Reading of Sir Gawain and the Green Knight* (London: R. & K. Paul, 1965), pp. 42–44, who also emphasizes the thematic importance of *trawþe* in the poem.

2. Quotations throughout are from *Sir Gawain and the Green Knight*, edited by J. R. R. Tolkien and E. V. Gordon, and revised by Norman Davis, 2nd ed. (Oxford: Clarendon, 1967).

3. This conflict is discussed at length by A. C. Spearing, *The Gawain-Poet: A Critical Study* (Cambridge: Cambridge University Press, 1970), pp. 198–212.

4. See my articles "*Sapientia et Fortitudo* as the Controlling Theme of *Beowulf*," *Studies in Philology* 55 (1958): 423–56; "*Beowulf*," in *Critical Approaches to Six Major English Works: Beowulf through Paradise Lost*, edited by R. M. Lumiansky and Herschel Baker (Philadelphia: University of Pennsylvania Press, 1968), pp. 3–40; and "*Sapientia et Fortitudo* in the Old English *Judith*," in *The Wisdom of Poetry: Essays in Early English Literature in Honor of Morton W. Bloomfield*, edited by Larry D. Benson and Siegfried Wenzel (Kalamazoo, Mich.: Medieval Institute Publications, Western Michigan University, 1982), pp. 13–29 and 264–68. This heroic ideal has recently been applied to *Sir Gawain* by Louis Blenkner, O.S.B., "Sin, Psychology, and the Structure of *Sir Gawain and the Green Knight*," *Studies in Philology* 74 (1977): 354–87.

5. For example Augustine, *De libero arbitrio*, III, xvii, 48, edited by William M. Green (CCL, 29; Turnhout, 1970), pp. 303–4; and *De Genesi ad litteram*, XI, xv, edited by Joseph Zycha (CSEL, 28, 1; Vienna, 1894), 1:347.

6. My argument thus far is paralleled, with further references, by David Farley Hills, "Gawain's Fault in *Sir Gawain and the Green Knight*," *Review of English Studies* 14 (1963): 124–31. An attractive explanation of *cowardyse* and *couetyse* by Theodore Silverstein, "Sir Gawain in a Dilemma, or Keeping Faith with Marcus Tullius Cicero," *Modern Philology* 75 (1977): 11–14, came to my attention after the present study was essentially completed.

7. Jerome, *Epistola C*, 3 (*PL* 22, col. 815); and especially Guilielmus

Peraldus, *Summae virtutum ac vitiorum*, I, III, ii, 6 (Cologne, 1629), 1: 176–77: "Et notandum quod secundum communem modum loquendi, & secundum modum etiam loquendi quem habet sacra scriptura, insipientia, vel imprudentia, vel stultitia non solum pertinent ad intellectum, sed etiam ad voluntatem & operationem. Vnde stultus est omnis peccator: & maxima stultitia est peccare, & maxima sapientia recte viuere. . . . Et notandum quod qui mortaliter peccat, multum stulte agit. . . . Sic nullus sapiens reputandus est qui in mortali peccato est. . . . Hic discernit vere inter sapientes & stultos, quod sapientes vadunt ad vitam æternam: Stulti vero ad mortem æternam." Note also the connections between *avaritia* and *stultitia*, ibid., II, IV, i, 7 (II, 51, 53, 58, 60–61).

8. "The Significance of the Hunting Scenes in *Sir Gawain and the Green Knight*," *Journal of English and Germanic Philology* 27 (1928): 1–15. For subsequent interpretations, see Avril Henry, "Temptation and Hunt in *Sir Gawain and the Green Knight*," *Medium Ævum* 45 (1976): 187–88 and 198, nn. 1–10, with Henry's own interpretation on pp. 188ff.; and more recently Blenkner, "Sin, Psychology, and Structure," pp. 361–65 *et passim*, and "The Three Hunts and Sir Gawain's Triple Fault," *American Benedictine Review* 29 (1978): 227–46, and Margaret Charlotte Ward, "French Ovidian Beasts in *Sir Gawain and the Green Knight*," *Neuphilologische Mitteilungen* 79 (1978): 152–61.

9. Thomas Cantimpratensis, *Liber de natura rerum*, IV, 30, edited by H. Boese (Berlin: De Gruyter, 1973), I, 125. A couplet of Martial, quoted by Thomas (ibid.) from Isidore, contrasts the defenselessness of the doe with the fierceness of the boar: "Dente timetur aper, defendunt cornua cervum: / Imbelles damme quid nisi preda sumus?"

10. Ps.-Hugh of St. Victor, *De bestiis et aliis rebus*, III, 17 (*PL* 177, col. 89). See also Isidore, *Etymologiae*, XII, i, 22, edited by W. M. Lindsay (Oxford: Clarendon, 1911).

11. Rabanus Maurus, *De universo*, VIII, 1 (*PL* 111, col. 225): "Vulpes dicta, quasi volupes. Est enim volubilibus pedibus, et nunquam rectis itineribus, sed tortuosis anfractibus currit: fraudulentum animal insidiisque decipiens. . . . Vulpes enim mystice . . . peccatorem hominem significat."

12. *MED*, B.5, pp. 1184–85, "britnen v.," especially 1 (c); and "britten v."

13. *Purgatorio*, XII, 61–63, edited by Giorgio Petrocchi, *La Commedia secondo l'antica vulgata* (Le opere di Dante Alighieri, Edizione Nazionale a cura della Società Dantesca Italiana, 7; Milan, 1966–67), III, 199: "Vedeva Troia in cenere e in caverne; / o Ilïón, come te basso e vile / mostrava il segno che lì si discerne!"

14. See particularly *De Genes. ad litt.*, XI, xv (above, n. 5), discussing the relation between Ecclesiasticus 10:15, "Initium omnis peccati super-

bia," and I Timothy 6:10, "Radix omnium malorum est avaritia [*Vulgate* cupiditas]."

15. *The Book of Vices and Virtues*, edited by W. Nelson Francis (EETS, 217; London, 1942), p. 13, offers a connection between pride and *vntrewþe*: "Þe first braunche of pride, þat is vntrewþe. . . ."

16. For example by Burrow, *A Reading*, pp. 104–10, who maintains that the confession must be invalid; his analysis of the "confession" to the Green Knight is on pp. 127–33.

17. For a convenient survey, see Robert G. Cook, "The Play-Element in *Sir Gawain and the Green Knight*," *Tulane Studies in English* 13 (1963): 5–31.

18. See especially Robert W. Ackerman, "Gawain's Shield: Penitential Doctrine in *Gawain and the Green Knight*," *Anglia* 76 (1958): 254–65; Richard H. Green, "Gawain's Shield and the Quest for Perfection," *ELH: A Journal of English Literary History* 29 (1962): 121–39; and Silverstein, "Sir Gawain in a Dilemma," pp. 1–8.

19. IV, vii, 14–15, edited by G. Busnelli and G. Vandelli (2nd ed.; Florence: Le Monnier, 1964), II, 79–80. For a full discussion of the number five, see Petrus Bungus (Pietro Bongo), *Numerorum mysteria* (Paris, 1618), pp. 249–64, and Appendix, pp. 24–25; and Green, "Gawain's Shield," pp. 129–35.

20. See for example Gregory, *Moralia in Iob*, II, xlvi, 71, on Job 1:13–15 (*PL* 75, col. 588): "Quæ profecto sapientia, nostra fides est. . . ."

21. *M. Roberti Holkoth . . . in Librum Sapientiæ . . . prælectiones CCXIII*, lect. 36, edited by Jacob Ryter ([Basel], 1586), p. 127; his reference is to the early ninth-century *Historia Brittonum* attributed to Nennius. Holkot's passage is paraphrased in an English sermon of the late fourteenth or early fifteenth century, edited by Woodburn O. Ross, *Middle English Sermons Edited from British Museum MS. Royal 18 B.xxiii*, sermon 49 (EETS, 209; London, 1940), pp. 325–26: "I rede in Gest*is* Britonu*m*, *et* recitat doctor Holcote sup*er* libru*m* Sapie*n*cie, þat Kyng Artoure had in þe innare parte of ys shelde and ymage of Oure Lady Mary deprented, beryng a child in her armes, þe wiche ymage he wold behold when þat he was werry in batell *and* feynte; and ano*n* for conforte *and* hope þat he had in hur*e* he waxed freshe *and* herty aȝeyn *and* in als good poynte for to feyȝthe as he was at þe begynnyng. Ryght so in þe same wyze þou þat arte in batell her*e* on erthe *and* fyȝthynge not only aȝeyns bodely enmyes but also aȝeyns goostely, þat is þe world, þe feend, *and* þin own fleshe, þer-for loke þat þou haue Marye, Goddis modur, in þe innare parte of þi sheld, þat is þi feyȝth *and* þin beleue." I am indebted for this reference to Edward C. Schweitzer of Louisiana State University.

22. Man's five fingers are allegorized by the fourteenth-century encyclopedist John of San Gimignano, *Summa de exemplis et rerum similitudini-*

bus, VI, xlviii (Venice, 1577), fol. 245^{r-v}, as the four Cardinal Virtues plus obedience (noted by Green, "Gawain's Shield," p. 134).

23. Note for example the inclusion of *charitas*, *mansuetudo*, and *castitas* among the "fruits of the spirit" in Galatians 5:22–23; and the progression from *pietas* to *fraternitatis amor* to *charitas* in II Peter 1:7. Peraldus, in the *Summa virtutum*, I, II, iv, "De charitate," offers possible connections between charity and each of our five virtues (italics mine): *Fraunchyse*: "Benigna etiam debet esse charitas, id est *egenis larga*. . . . Duobus primis facit Charitas, vt bene nos habeamus in his, quæ nostra sunt, mala propria patienter portando, & *bona propria liberaliter largiendo* [ch. 2; I, 124]." *Fela3schyp*: "Tertio [potest incitare ad amorem proximi] *fraternitas naturalis* quæ est inter omnes homines. . . . Quarto *fraternitas spiritualis* . . . [ch. 8; I, 139]." *Clannes*: "Tria hic tanguntur quæ ad charitatem disponunt: [Fides, spes, et] *puritas cordis* [ch. 1; I, 119]. . . . Antiquus inimicus *castitatem* in nobis si sine charitate viderit, non timet: quia ipse carne non premitur, vt luxuria dissoluatur [ch. 2; I, 124]." *Cortaysye*: "Charitas enim . . . pretiositas est hominis & operum ipsius. . . . Primum [quod valere potest ad hoc vt aliquis ametur a proximo] est *modestia in sermone* [ch. 9; I, 140]." *Pité*: "Charitas Dei & proximi propria & specialis virtus est *piorum* atque sanctorum, quum cæteræ virtutes bonis & malis possint esse communes [ch. 2; I, 123]."

24. Larry D. Benson, *Art and Tradition in Sir Gawain and the Green Knight* (New Brunswick, N.J.: Rutgers University Press, 1965), pp. 58–95. For the "green man," see now Kathleen Basford, *The Green Man* (Cambridge: D. S. Brewer, 1978); and for a recent study of the "wild man," Timothy Husband and Gloria Gilmore-House, *The Wild Man: Medieval Myth and Symbolism* (New York: The Metropolitan Museum of Art, 1980). A medieval stone sculpture of a bearded man holding an ax is preserved in the south transept of the Priory Church of St. Seiriol at Penmon on the Isle of Anglesey; Royal Commission on Ancient and Historical Monuments in Wales and Monmouthshire, *An Inventory of the Ancient Monuments in Anglesey* (London, 1937), pl. 79, upper right, and p. 121.

25. *Sir Gawain and the Green Knight: An Essay in Interpretation*, Cooper Monographs on English and American Language and Literature, 6 (Bern, 1961), pp. 59–60.

26. Howard R. Patch, *The Goddess Fortuna in Mediaeval Literature* (Cambridge: Harvard University Press, 1927), p. 43 and n. 4.

27. Lines 15853–59, edited by Gottlob Heinrich Friedrich Scholl, *Diu Crône von Heinrîch von dem Türlîn* (Bibliothek des Litterarischen Vereins in Stuttgart, 27; Stuttgart, 1852), pp. 194–95.

28. First proposed in a paper read at meetings in 1957 and 1958 by Alfred L. Kellogg and summarized by Donald R. Howard, *The Three Temp-*

tations: Medieval Man in Search of the World (Princeton: Princeton University Press, 1966), pp. 232–34. I would suggest, however, that the three Biblical evils are reflected in the poem not by Gawain's temptations on the three successive days but by the three different temptations offered him—with *concupiscentia carnis* dramatized by the lady's offer of her body, *concupiscentia oculorum* (which is traditionally interpreted as avarice) by her offer of the gold ring (1813–20), and *superbia vitae* by her offer of the supposedly life-protecting girdle.

III

Forms and Functions of Latin Speech, 400–800

George A. Kennedy
The University of North Carolina at Chapel Hill

Although people have been known to paint pictures, mold figures, or create a variety of sound with strings or pipes or drums, or upon occasion to jump up and down and beat their breasts, the characteristic form of human communication is intelligible speech. A certain philosopher once observed that man is a political animal, and political institutions give form to the development of conventions in speech. Speech is sometimes expressive, sometimes informative, sometimes impressive; it has some purpose, whether to express how happy or unhappy the speaker is or to convey information or to impress another with the need to believe something or to do something. The technique by which a speaker seeks to accomplish his purpose is rhetoric, in the primary sense of that word. Since the word "rhetoric" is variously used or misused, it is important to stress that the term will here be used in its original, primary, and broadest sense. Techniques of written composition or devices of style are a branch of rhetoric, but only one of several branches.

In most societies, throughout most of history, effective rhetoric has been learned by observation, imitation, and experimentation. This is as true in Rome or in Paris as in Bali or Madagascar. Such techniques can be described and analyzed as a system of rhetoric, but conceptualization, and thus the systematic teaching of rhetorical theory, is characteristic only of the most advanced societies, and not all of them. Even in China and India the conceptualization of rhetoric was rather limited. Only in Greece in the fifth century before Christ was there a full attempt to make rhetoric

[45]

a conscious art that could be taught and learned. The reasons for this unique development lie outside the subject of this paper, though it can be said that they were closely associated with a wider movement toward conceptualization which constituted the birth of philosophy and, with the political needs of Greek polity, especially democracy. One result of the practical context of Greek rhetoric was to give the subject a strong judicial cast; rhetoric was directed toward meeting the needs of speakers in a court of law and to a lesser extent in public assemblies or later in the imperial courts. As we shall see, this judicial focus persisted as a characteristic of classical rhetorical theory even in the Middle Ages. In addition to its primary uses in public address, classical rhetoric had some impact on individual communication, as in dialectic, and was adapted to writing at least by the fourth century before Christ.[1]

In the various societies of the Middle Ages, as in any other human society, oral communication played a role, but despite the decline of literacy,[2] the general view is that writing became more important than speech. Except for some kinds of preaching and theological disputation, formal speech is usually not regarded as an effective form of persuasion in the Middle Ages, and men's minds and actions were largely manipulated by a rhetoric of brute force, authority, or promises of rewards and threats of punishment in this world or the next and not by logical argument. The most striking development is the use of various forms of ordeal—boiling water, the cross, or combat—or of the oath of compurgation as procedures in Germanic courts of law, replacing rational argumentation based on evidence as established by Roman law. Classical rhetoric could deal only with probabilities; the new procedures could reveal the certainty of truth as known to God. The theory of rhetoric conceptualized in classical times for use in the courts and senates is said by Ernst Robert Curtius to have been of no use in the Middle Ages,[3] and thus it is assumed to have been studied for its application to written forms of communication. To most medievalists, rhetoric probably does not mean an art of persuasion but one of three other things: a part of the trivium, usually falling between grammar and dialectic[4] and taught for its value as general education or scriptural exegesis; that system of composition set forth in treatises on *dictamen* for prose or in *artes poetriae* for verse; or—and here alone an oral application is thought to flourish—in handbooks on preaching, where it is perhaps as strongly influenced by dialectic as by rhetoric.[5] My intention here is not to refute this picture of medieval rhetoric but to complement and extend it by a consideration of oral forms up to the time of Charlemagne. The study could and should be extended through the rest of medieval history.

Rhetoric as taught in the trivium was primarily the theory of invention, including the elaborate doctrine of the *status* or *constitutiones* or issues of judicial oratory, and secondarily the theory of style. The emphasis is clear both from the early compendia of rhetoric and from the commentaries on Cicero written in late antiquity and in the second half of the Middle Ages.[6] A major authority on rhetoric was Cicero's *De Inventione*, which is devoted solely to invention and deals in large part with *status* theory. Furthermore, its companion work, *Rhetorica ad Herennium*, which was also attributed to Cicero in the Middle Ages, was by no means studied solely for its fourth book on style. The figures of speech, the best understood aspect of style in the Middle Ages, were often regarded as matters of grammar rather than rhetoric and had indeed often been treated as such by grammarians of later antiquity. The most influential discussion of tropes and figures was the *Barbarismus* of Donatus, which is a part of a larger grammatical treatise. Bede's little work on tropes and figures is derived from Donatus and belongs in the grammatical tradition. Conversely, rules of versification, which in classical times were a part of grammar, in the Middle Ages were sometimes thought of as a part of rhetoric. For example, when Gregory of Tours at the end of his *History of the Franks* expresses the hope that his successors as bishop, unlike himself, will know the seven arts, he includes rhetoric—and calls it the art of versification.[7] No technical discussion of rhetoric from the early Middle Ages includes metrics, and Gregory's usage is perhaps a popular one: another instance of the popular misidentifications of rhetoric to be found throughout history.

In general, the position can be supported that to most *early* medieval scholars who had studied it, rhetoric meant the planning of a prosecution or defense for presentation in a court of law or of a speech for some public occasion. Though they may have expected secondary benefits from its study, such as a better understanding of the eloquence of the Scriptures, as classicists claim that the study of Latin contributes to a better understanding of English, it seems perverse to believe that medieval scholars did not expect to teach or learn something immediately applicable when they turned to the study of rhetoric, just as the primary goal of the study of Latin remains the ability to read Latin. Indeed, the study of rhetoric has always been related to the need for speech; the art was conceptualized in the first place in Greece for use in the lawcourts and continued to be taught for that purpose through the time of the Roman empire. Its rebirth in the later Middle Ages and in the Renaissance was directly related to the civic life of the Italian states; its flowering in the seventeenth and eighteenth centuries in France and England primarily resulted from the increased opportunities for discourse in pulpit, in senate, and at the bar; and the progress of rhetorical studies in the twentieth century is closely related to new forms and new opportunities of communication. From study of the history of rhetoric, it would be an a priori assumption that rhetoric as a discipline survived into the Middle Ages because it was useful in speech. We need to see to what extent this is substantiated.

In the fourth and fifth centuries of the Christian era, the fabric of Roman society was still partly intact around the western Mediterranean despite barbarian invasions, and the forms of civic speech were those that had existed for centuries. Rhetorical schools, as preparation for public life, flourished in Italy, Gaul, Spain, and Africa as a secondary stage of education after grammar.[8] Teachers were nominated by public officials, as Augustine for example was nominated by Symmachus to the chair of rhetoric in Milan,[9] and were paid by municipal funds. It appears from Sidonius Apollinaris (*Epist.* 4.3.10) that municipal chairs were still in existence in some Gallic cities in the second half of the fifth century. In Italy they lasted into the sixth with the encouragement of the Ostrogothic kings. Athalaric, for example, who reigned from 526 to 534, once complained to the senate that *doctores elo-quentiae Romanae* were not being paid their proper salary (Cassio-dorus, *Variae* 9.21). The last known public teacher of rhetoric in Rome is Melior Felix in 534,[10] though Justinian made an effort in 554 to reestablish municipal chairs in Rome when it was under Byzantine rule.[11] Private instruction in grammar and some aspects of rhetoric continued in some cities. There is sporadic evidence for Rome, Ravenna, and elsewhere throughout the early Middle Ages.[12]

The theory of rhetoric taught in these schools is summarized in the handbooks by the writers we call the *Rhetores Latini Minores*, including Julius Victor and Fortunatianus, and in the encyclopedic work of Martianus Capella. In general, the system does not differ greatly from the rhetorical theory of Cicero or Quintilian, both of whom were regarded as higher authorities, but there seems to be an increased emphasis on *status* theory, and interest in memory and delivery as parts of rhetoric faded, suggesting the disappearance of opportunities for a speech of summation in court trials.[13] Much of the time of students in late antique schools still went into the composition of declamations of the sort practiced since the time of the elder Seneca, either the deliberative exercises known as *suasoriae* or the judicial exercises called *controversiae*, with their imaginary laws and their tyrants, pirates, and ravished maidens to keep the students interested. Some of the declamations attributed to Quintilian were perhaps composed as models by a teacher of rhetoric as late as the fourth century. The last surviving declamations are those by Ennodius, later bishop of Pavia, which were composed for several young protégés in the school of Deuterius at Milan in the first decade of the sixth century.[14] The brief works of Emporius on ethopoeia, commonplaces, and materials for deliberative and demonstrative oratory also seem to reflect the declamations of the schools. Emporius cannot be precisely dated, but the early sixth century is the latest likely date.[15] There is no clear sign of the practice of declamation after the middle of the sixth century. Priscian's *Praeexercitamina*, a translation of the work on introductory exercises attributed to Hermogenes, had some currency in the West, though it was made in Constantinople in the early years of the sixth century and reflects the strength of rhetorical education in the East which survived throughout the medieval period. But Priscian's exercises are primarily associated with grammatical studies. They do not include declamation, though they do include some techniques that had been used in declamation, such as *locus communis*, *laus*, and *comparatio*. After the mid-sixth century the application of these techniques was chiefly in the writing of poetry, where they can be seen for example in poems by Eugenius, bishop of Toledo from 646 to 658.[16]

It is interesting that the one passage from the early Middle Ages which comes closest to describing declamation is also from the Visigothic kingdom, which enjoyed closer ties with Byzantium than did many other parts of the West. This is the passage describing ethopoeia in Isidore of Seville (2.14): "When portrayal of a pirate is undertaken, the speech will be bold, abrupt, and daring; when the speech of a woman is simulated, the expression should be suited to her sex. In the case of a young man or an old man or a soldier or a general or a parasite or a farmer or a philosopher a different kind of speech must be employed for each." These are the characters of declamation as seen in Seneca the Elder or Quintilian. They are not unlike characters of Roman comedy or elegy, and some reappear in medieval arts of poetry and in the rules for *dictamen* as described by Alberic of Monte Cassino (7.1) and others. It seems likely that Isidore knew ethopoeia from literary sources and envisioned its use in written composition and that the passage does not prove oral declamation to have been practiced in the Spanish schools of his time,[17] though Isidore may have known that declamation still existed in Byzantine ruled portions of the empire. Latin declamation thus probably disappeared with the collapse of municipal schools at the end of the fifth century in many parts of the empire[18] and by the middle of the sixth century in Italy. It reappeared, however, in the tenth century, perhaps through the efforts of Gerbert, and thereafter there are occasional references to declamation throughout the medieval and renaissance periods.[19]

From this background we may turn to the only overall account of classical rhetorical theory surviving from the sixth century, that in Cassiodorus' *Institutiones Divinae et Humanae*, probably written between 550 and 560. In his preface Cassiodorus tells how he had tried to get Pope Agapetus (who reigned from 535 to 536) to establish Christian schools in Rome, where, he says, secular schools were "swarming with students." His hopes were foiled by the wars that raged through Italy, surely the invasion of Belisarius and the 537 siege of Rome. Instead, from his monastery at Vivarium, Cassiodorus, as he puts it, "was driven by divine charity to this device, namely, in the place of a teacher to prepare for you [he addresses the monks of his monastery] under the Lord's guidance these introductory books; through which, in my opinion, the unbroken line of the Divine Scriptures and the compendious knowledge of secular letters might with the Lord's beneficence be related." (1.*pr*.1).[20] A justification for the study of a subject such as rhetoric is given in greater detail in chapter twenty-seven of Book One, where we are told that "we can understand much in sacred literature as well as in the most learned interpreters through figures of speech, much through definitions, much through the art of grammar, much through the art of rhetoric, etc." Figures of speech are mentioned separately from both grammar and rhetoric. The authority for studying rhetoric as a basis of interpretation of the Scriptures stems from Augustine's *De Doctrina Christiana*, and how Cassiodorus envisioned it to be carried out can be seen in his own commentary on the Psalms.[21]

Cassiodorus devotes Book Two of his work to secular knowledge. The account of grammar comes first, largely drawn from Donatus. Cassiodorus mentions figures of speech as common to grammarians and orators and refers the readers for detail to a codex he has prepared containing works on grammar and figures. There follows the chapter on rhetoric: its definition as expertness in discourse in civil questions; its traditional parts—invention, arrangement, style, memory, and delivery; the kinds of oratory—demonstrative, deliberative, and judicial; and then, treated in somewhat greater detail, the theory of the *status* of judicial cases. Cases, we are told, revolve around legal or rational issues. In the latter instance there are four kinds of cases, as described by Cicero in *De Inventione*: *coniecturalis* or fact; *finis* or definition; *qualitas* or quality; and *translatio* or jurisdiction of the court. Then comes a list of the parts of the judicial oration and a discussion of rhetorical argumentation, both inductive and deductive, with a few words on memory and delivery at the end.

Since Cassiodorus was a major source for subsequent writers, his picture of rhetoric deserves serious attention. It has several remarkable features. First, rhetoric is clearly a civic art; its function is persuasion and especially persuasion in the lawcourts for which the student is taught the various forms of conflict of issue and forms of proof. Second, style is mentioned, but it is not discussed as a part of rhetoric.[22] Nothing is said about the application of rhetoric to the writing of verse. Third, in the discussion of rhetoric there are only occasional references to a Christian context, to which Cassiodorus might be expected to adapt his teaching. His work seems to have undergone revision, signs of which are preserved in the manuscript tradition. One family of manuscripts, representing one stage of revision, cites Psalm 28 as an example of demonstrative oratory.[23] In all manuscripts the subdivision of *status* theory called *confessio* is defined as "the position in which the accused does not defend that which had been done, but begs to be pardonned; we have pointed out that this has to do with penitents."[24] In addition, Cassiodorus recommends that monks read the account of memory and delivery in Fortunatianus, which he has incorporated in a codex together with Cicero's *De Inventione* and Quintilian (2.2.10). "The monk will derive a certain advantage from this book, since it seems not improper for him to adapt to his own uses that which orators have profitably applied to disputation. Duly cautious, he will pay heed to memorization, as applied to divine reading, when he has learned its force and nature from the aforementioned book; he will foster the art of delivery in reading the divine law aloud; and he will, moreover, preserve a careful manner of speaking in chanting the psalms. Thus, though he be somewhat occupied with secular books, he will be restored to holy work upon the completion of his instruction" (2.2.16).[25] Monks did not preach, and the potential application of rhetoric to preaching is not mentioned by Cassiodorus, though it is perhaps implicit in the contribution of rhetoric to scriptural exegesis and might be

The System of Rhetoric as Set Forth by Cassiodorus, Institutiones II.2

Section

1. Definition: ars autem rethorica est, sicut magristri tradunt saecularium litterarum, bene dicendi scientia in civilibus quaestionibus.

2. Parts: inventio, dispositio, elocutio, memoria, pronuntiatio.

3. Genera causarum rethoricae sunt tria principalia: demonstrativum, deliberativum, iudiciale.

4. Status vero dicitur ea res in qua causa consistit; fit autem ex intentione et depulsione. status causarum aut rationales sunt aut legale. rationales secundum generales quaestiones IIII:

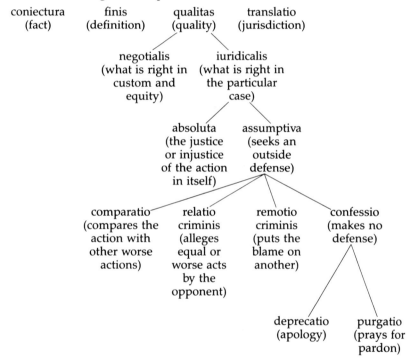

coniectura	finis	qualitas	translatio
(fact)	(definition)	(quality)	(jurisdiction)

negotialis (what is right in custom and equity) — iuridicalis (what is right in the particular case)

absoluta (the justice or injustice of the action in itself) — assumptiva (seeks an outside defense)

comparatio (compares the action with other worse actions) — relatio criminis (alleges equal or worse acts by the opponent) — remotio criminis (puts the blame on another) — confessio (makes no defense)

deprecatio (apology) — purgatio (prays for pardon)

11. Rethorica argumentatio ita tractatur:

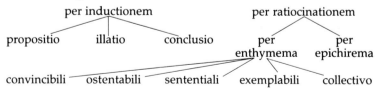

per inductionem — per ratiocinationem

propositio — illatio — conclusio — per enthymema — per epichirema

convincibili — ostentabili — sententiali — exemplabili — collectivo

[53]

seen also in the elaboration of deliberative oratory in one family of manuscripts to include "what to seek, what to shun, what to teach, what to prohibit."[26]

Cassiodorus had not only been thoroughly trained in classical rhetoric in his youth but before his withdrawal from public life had had the kind of public career that classical teachers of rhetoric envisioned for their students, as we can see from his *Variae*, a collection of letters written for the Ostrogothic court. Although, while writing the *Institutiones* years later, Cassiodorus was clearly aware of great political and military upheavals, it did not occur to him that the art of civic discourse had been rendered useless. It should be remembered that Cassiodorus in the southern tip of Italy was living under Byzantine rule and thus under Roman law and procedure, even if at times regular procedures could not be observed.

Was there any potential application for the inventional rhetoric described by Cassiodorus in other parts of the West? In northern Italy the Lombards brought with them a singularly barbaric legal tradition that seems to have offered little occasion for judicial rhetoric and substituted trial by oath or combat for debate.[27] A reading of the *History of the Lombards* by Paul the Deacon, written in the late eighth century, does not suggest much place for judicial rhetoric, though Paul occasionally mentions individuals as having studied the liberal arts.[28] Judicial conditions in Gaul were somewhat better, though Merovingian codes also provided for ordeal.[29] It was chiefly in the church that something like the conditions of Roman courts survived. Our best source on speech in Merovingian times is Gregory of Tours's *History of the Franks*, complemented by some references to rhetorical studies found in Fortunatus, a poet who employs all the techniques of classical rhetoric in his works. Let us examine Gregory's account of a trial in which he himself participated and consider how the issues and techniques may be analyzed in terms of the inventional rhetoric described by Cassiodorus. A partial model for such an approach is offered by letter 201 of Gerbert, later Pope Sylvester II, to Wilderode of Strasbourg in 995, in which he describes the trial of Arnulf and the legal, logical, and rhetorical issues it involved.[30] The approach is probably worthy of imitation in the case of other examples of medieval discourse.

In A.D. 577 Praetextatus, bishop of Rouen, was accused by King Chilperic of plotting against him, specifically of using money from property of Queen Brunhilda (widow of King Sigibert and at this time wife of Chilperic's son Merovech) to buy support for Merovech against his father. As reported by Gregory in the long eighteenth chapter of Book Five of the *History of the Franks*,[31] Praetextatus was first given a preliminary hearing before the king as though before a Roman magistrate and then was held for trial by a council of bishops convened at Paris.[32] At the trial the king acted as prosecutor. The charges were three in number. First, that, in violation of canon law, Praetextatus had officiated at the marriage of Merovech and Brunhilda. This charge is not discussed in Gregory's account but helps to show the tie between Praetextatus and Merovech and to undermine Praetextatus' position, something regularly done by Roman orators. The second charge was that Praetextatus had conspired with Merovech to kill King Chilperic. Third, that he had given money to other people and urged them to support Merovech. At this point the crowd outside the church, perhaps organized by Chilperic's men to do so, tried to break in and lynch Praetextatus but was restrained. Some of the bishops were doubtless intimidated by the event, which in classical rhetoric would be regarded as an external mode of persuasion. The fact that the king had the crowd restrained contributes to his ethos; that is, it suggests that he is a just and law-abiding ruler.

Praetextatus denies the charges made against him. In the system of inventional rhetoric as described by Cassiodorus (2.2.5) that means that he first used the *status coniecturae* or the issue of fact. In reply, witnesses were introduced who had articles of value that they said Praetextatus had given them to support Merovech. Use of witnesses is the commonest form of external evidence in classical rhetoric. Gregory says the witnesses were lying; if so they may have been bribed or otherwise constrained. Bribery of witnesses is a regular topic of classical judicial oratory from the earliest Greek times, but it is hard to substantiate and is often indiscriminately alleged. Praetextatus at this point admits the fact of the gifts but claims they were given in return for horses and other things he had received from the witnesses. By his admission he shifts the issue from *status coniecturae* to *status finis*. It is now his defense that the act should not be defined as bribery but as legal recompense.

At this point the king left, and the council met in executive session. Aetius, archdeacon of Paris, arrives and argues that it is in the interests of the bishops to support another bishop. Although his argument is legally *extra causam*, it is powerful. It also takes the form of an enthymeme. In the usage of the time this means that it is a logical argument based on probability, one premiss of which is implied rather than expressed. Cassiodorus identifies five kinds of enthymemes (2.2.13), and that used by Aetius might be said to fall into the class he calls "sententious," for it is based on a general truth: it is in the general interest of bishops to support another bishop. Gregory then speaks and urges the king's friends among the clergy to restrain the king. He begins with a quotation from Ezekiel (33:6): "If the watchman shall see the iniquity of a man and not declare it, he shall be guilty for a lost soul." This is made an authoritative premiss for what Cassiodorus calls an *ostentabile*, or demonstrative, enthymeme with the conclusion: "Therefore, do not be silent, but speak and place the king's sins before his eyes." Gregory seeks to support this with an inductive argument that Cassiodorus, in a rather confused discussion (2.2.11), had described as "a statement which by the use of clearly known particulars seeks to gain approval for the generalization with which the induction was begun."[33] That is to say, it uses examples. Gregory's examples are what happened when Chlodomer seized Sigismund and when the emperor Maximus forced Saint Martin to give communion to a bishop who was a homicide. The force of the argument is to transfer responsibility for protection from the king himself to the bishops. Such a transfer is a form of *status qualitatis*, known in Cassiodorus' system as *remotio criminis* or removal of the charge, itself a subdivision of *status assumptivus*, which is a subdivision of *status iuridicalis*, which in turn is a subdivision of *status qualitatis* (2.2.4–5).

The trial is then adjourned for the night and the king summons Gregory to appear before him. The scene has been carefully set to resemble a church; the king stands beside a *tabernaculum ex ramis factum* with the bishop of Bordeaux on his right and the bishop of Paris on his left. Before the three figures, threatening but also offering absolution, there is an altar-like table, set with bread and wine.[34] The king immediately accuses Gregory of speaking unjustly and supports his argument with a maxim: "A crow does not tear out the eye of another crow." The use of maxims or proverbs is a traditional device of classical rhetoric, though not noted by Cassiodorus. Gregory replies that the king can correct injustice in others but who can correct injustice in the king? This is *comparatio* in Cassiodorus' system (2.2.13). The king then threatens to stir up the people of Tours against Gregory; in other words he again invokes an argument *extra causam*. Gregory counters with a charge of injustice against the king, a *relatio criminis* in Cassiodorus. He says the king should observe *legem et canones*. Chilperic then tries to calm Gregory and offers him food, another external device. It is becoming clear that the would-be autocratic Germanic king regularly appeals to nonrational arguments external to the case, while the bishop, living under Roman law and Christian principles, seeks to employ rational and legal proofs. Gregory says that it is more important to do God's will and be just than to eat. He asks the king not to neglect the law and the canons. Then he will be regarded as just, an *enthymema ostentabile*. The king seems to agree, and Gregory eats bread and drinks wine.

In the night messengers of Queen Fredegunda (wife of Chilperic and an enemy of Merovech, who is not her son) come to Gregory and try to bribe him to vote against Praetextatus. He gives an ambiguous answer. Other bishops are similarly approached.

The next day the trial is resumed by the king before the council. The king cites the canon that a bishop guilty of theft shall be cast from office. Gregory asks whom he has in mind. The king replies that Praetextatus has stolen two cases of costly articles. Praetextatus again uses *status finis* or definition. The articles were on deposit with him from Queen Brunhilda, he claims, and he reminds the king of an earlier conversation in which the king seemed to accept that point. The king responds to the issue of definition by saying that the articles could not be for safekeeping, since Praetextatus has cut up a girdle of gold and used the parts to bribe men to drive out the king. This is an enthymeme, employing a sign, the cutting of the girdle. At this point Praetextatus admits the fact but denies the intent. That is, he shifts from *status finis* to *status qualitatis*. He is thus gradually being driven through the sequence of *status* as taught in the rhetorical schools and discussed by Cassiodorus some twenty years earlier. He claims that he has a right to use the articles since they are property of Merovech and that Merovech is his spiritual son—he had baptized him.

To a modern reader this might seem a weak argument, but Gregory regards it as very strong before an ecclesiastical court and apparently the king did as well. He confers with his advisers and tells them he is losing the case. He deputizes them to talk with Praetextatus privately and counsel him to confess the charge and throw himself on the king's mercy. A scene will be planned in which the king's friends will throw themselves at the king's feet and ask him to pardon Praetextatus. It is implied that he will be forgiven. Praetextatus is thus offered what seems an easy solution, while the king seeks to establish a situation in which he will be in control.

The next day the trial is resumed. The king asks Praetextatus why, if the gifts were in return for other gifts, he had demanded an oath of fidelity to Merovech from the recipients, another enthymeme with a sign. Somewhere in Chilperic's entourage there is clearly someone briefing him about the use of evidence. Praetextatus again replies that Merovech is his spiritual son. Gregory says that the dispute grew warmer, but gives no details. Finally, Praetextatus, as suggested by the king's friends, throws himself on the ground and cries, "I have sinned against heaven and before you, most merciful king; I am a wicked homicide; I wished to kill you and raise your son to the throne." *Confessio* is a final form of *status* of quality in Cassiodorus' system (2.2.5), as already noted. It takes two forms, either apology or, as here, *deprecatio* or prayer for pardon. The king then throws himself at the feet of the court—some place for *actio* still existed in sixth-century rhetoric even though that fifth and last part of rhetoric was neglected by most theorists, and Chilperic certainly had a fine sense of the dramatic. He cries, "Hear, most pious bishops, the defendant confesses his awful crime." Praetextatus is led away. The king withdraws and sends the court a book of canons with a "new quaternion" added which is labeled "apostolic canons," a flagrant rhetorical device. Included is the following: "Let a bishop detected in homicide, adultery, or perjury be cast from office." Praetextatus is brought back before the council and, in a daze, hears Bishop Bertram of Bordeaux, a tool of the king, declare that he cannot win the bishops' mercy until he has the king's indulgence. The king orders that Praetextatus' robes be torn off, that Psalm 108 be read over him as a curse, and that he be excommunicated forever. Gregory boldly objects on the ground that this exceeds the canon, but Praetextatus is led away. In the night he attempts to escape but is captured, beaten, and then exiled to an island. Merovech is soon afterward forced to suicide or possibly killed by an agent of Queen Fredegunda. In exile Praetextatus composed a collection of *orationes* that he later read to a gathering of brother bishops. According to Gregory (8.10), some liked them, some found them wanting in art. *Oratio* often means prayer in the sixth century, but the reference to art suggests that these were sermons and that they sought to employ rhetorical devices.[35] Eventually Praetextatus was restored to his throne (7.16), but he continued to quarrel with Queen Fredegunda, was finally stabbed in his own church by her agents, and died cursing the Queen (8.31).

The trial of Praetextatus can be read as a conflict of two rhetorics: King Chilperic seeks to accomplish his purposes primarily by the use of external means of proof, his own power and ability to manipulate scenes; Praetextatus and Gregory followed argument and appeal in the classical tradition as it survived in the church. Gregory never mentions Cassiodorus, and the earliest that we can identify manuscripts of his work as available in France is in the early ninth century.[36] I am not arguing that Praetextatus and Gregory were directly familiar with *status* theory as found in Cassiodorus. They may or may not have been, and it is possible that they simply employed conventions of argument traditionally used in ecclesiastical debate which they had learned from imitation.

Gregory mentions (10.31) Martianus Capella's work on the seven liberal arts, including rhetoric. Although he had probably not read it himself, some of his contemporaries certainly had. The closest I can find to a direct reference to knowledge of inventional rhetorical theory in sixth-century Gaul is the statement of Stephen of Auxerre in his life of Saint Amator which describes Amator as being trained in the doctrines of all the arts and the subtleties of disputation, including figures of poetical invention, enthymemes of rhetors, *nodos* and *aenigmata* of lawyers, and syllogistic questions of philosophers.[37] In any event, *status* theory continued to be applicable in the church and an account such as that given by Cassiodorus would have some utility to a student interested in understanding the techniques.

It should be noted, however, that the trial of Praetextatus does not seem to provide opportunity for prolonged oratory such as the cases in which Cicero and the younger Pliny won their fame in the classical period. There are no extended opening statements and no elaborate closing pleas. The procedure is basically one of interrogation, with question and answer. As noted above, jury trials in late antiquity seem already to have been developing in this direction and the function of judicial rhetoric had become not so much the writing of a speech as the arguing of a case. The situation in the Frankish court has taken the additional step of evolving *status* during the actual trial rather than planning it in advance as would ordinarily have been the case in classical times. An account of rhetoric such as that in Cassiodorus was appropriate for the procedures of his time and the following age, not only that it emphasized *status* and *argumentatio*, but also that it largely ignored devices of style, amplification, and delivery, which are chiefly useful when a litigant has an opportunity to speak without interruption.

After Cassiodorus the next discussion of *status* theory is that found in the second book of the *Etymologiae* of Isidore of Seville, written in the early seventh century. Why does Isidore stress *status* theory in his chapter on rhetoric? One answer, of course, is that it was a part of traditional knowledge that, whatever its utility, was of interest to an encyclopedist. Isidore's account is largely derived from Cassiodorus, and Cassiodorus' personal authority is perhaps also a factor. But there are signs that Isidore thought the system was somehow useful. His account of rhetorical invention is followed by a chapter on law (2.10), which seems to be a contribution of his own; such an insertion is found in no other discussion of rhetoric before this time. We are fortunate in knowing something about the Visigothic legal system,[38] and it is possible to say that at least in theory it constituted an orderly procedure for fair trial before judges. Isidore's definition of rhetoric, like that of Cassiodorus, is "a civic art" and his insertion of a chapter on the law thus suggests that in Spain in the seventh century some opportunities for judicial argumentation survived in civil courts, as well as in the church. Fontaine has briefly explored the possibilities that would probably repay further study.[39] Isidore's discussion, of course, greatly strengthened the tradition of inventional rhetoric and made it accessible to many in the later Middle Ages.

After Isidore there is no discussion of rhetorical invention for about 150 years. It reappears in a rather full form in Alcuin's *Dialogue* with Charlemagne, where its contemporary application is expressly noted. Alcuin explains the system, which he knows about chiefly from Cicero's *De Inventione* and Julius Victor, because Charlemagne, in the dialogue at least, wants to know about secular oratory in a judicial setting. Wallach has argued that Alcuin is seeking to educate Charlemagne in the art of kingship.[40] Even if this thesis is incorrect, and it has been questioned,[41] Wallach illustrates the contemporary judicial application of at least some of Alcuin's discussion.

Classical rhetoricians, followed by Cassiodorus and Isidore, distinguish three categories of public address: judicial, deliberative, and epideictic. We have examined the survival of judicial oratory in the early Middle Ages and may now turn briefly to the deliberative form. Deliberative oratory in the early Middle Ages means persuasion or dissuasion, either of a belief or of need for action (see Cassiodorus *Institutiones* 2.2.2; Isidore, *Etymologiae* 2.4.3–4). Although Aristotle (*Rhetoric* 1.1358b35) had seen the basis of decision in utility, Cicero (*De Inventione* 2.156) had redefined this as a combination of the advantageous and the just. His view commended itself to Christian writers.

There was, of course, relatively little free debate in late antiquity, though some can be found in the senates of Rome and Constantinople and to judge from Libanius also in local councils.[42] From historians like Ammianus Marcellinus we can see a variety of other occasions upon which a speaker urged a course of action: debate among advisers of kings or generals as to the best policy or strategy, addresses by generals to their troops before going into battle, and most important of all, speeches by ambassadors, both abroad and on their return home. To take one specific example, Cassiodorus' grandfather was sent by Valentinian III on an embassy to seek peace from Attila the Hun. In comparison, rhetorical challenges faced by Demosthenes or Cicero pale into insignificance, but as described by the younger Cassiodorus in a letter he wrote to the senate on behalf of Theodoric, the ambassador was entirely successful and credit is given to his rhetorical abilities:

> Calm in conscious strength, he despised all those terrible wrathful faces that scowled around him. He did not hesitate to meet the full force of the invectives of the madman who fancied himself about to grasp the empire of the world. He found the king insolent; he left him pacified; and so ably did he argue down all his slanderous pretexts for dispute, that though the Hun's interest was to quarrel with the richest empire in the world, he nevertheless condescended to seek its favor. The firmness of the orator roused the fainting courage of his countrymen, and men felt that Rome could not be pronounced defenseless while she was armed with such ambassadors.[43]

I would not want to vouch for the historicity of the details, but the letter shows clearly the continued belief in the power of speech that writers since Isocrates had celebrated. Gregory of Tours mentions many embassies and describes in detail (*History of the Franks* 9.20) one that he undertook for King Childebert to King Gunthram in 588. Although some embassies were simply proclamatory, it seems likely that an ambassador like Gregory had at least some latitude of speech, argumentation, and action. An even more celebrated embassy is that undertaken by Gregory the Great to Constantinople in the days of his political activity. Ambassadorial rhetoric in almost all periods of history, including the medieval, needs more study.

Another important opportunity for deliberative speech was furnished by councils and disputes of the church. Acts of councils often include an introductory letter setting forth the agenda or the text of a speech, the *tomus*, by an important official, and here is preserved a rhetorical form that deserves study as such. One example is the *Tome of the Most Holy Faith*, which is a version of the address by the Visigothic King Recared to the Third Council of Toledo in 589.[44] Recared's speech is his confession of orthodox faith on conversion from Arianism, with his request to the bishops to witness and implement the conversion of his nation as a result. Though largely proclamatory, it thus calls for some action and may be properly classified as a deliberative speech. The speech has some characteristics of classical rhetoric: it could, for example, be divided into *captatio benevolentiae*, narration, body of the message, and peroration, and there are tropes and figures of the classical sort, but the argumentation and topics are fundamentally Christian rather than classical.

There is not space here to describe in any detail the nature and historical development of Christian rhetoric as a distinct tradition. I have sought to do so elsewhere.[45] Fundamental sources are the fourth chapter of Exodus and the second, third, and fourth chapters of Second Corinthians. In Aristotelian rhetoric, which constitutes the philosophical base of the classical system, there are three modes of proof: *ethos* or the character of the speaker as inherent in the speech; *logos* or the rational argument of the speech developed through enthymemes, or deductive argument based on signs or premises, and inductive argument based on examples; and finally *pathos* or the moving of the emotions of the audience. In Christian rhetoric, briefly put, there is something corresponding to *ethos* in authority, either that of God or of the Scriptures and fathers of the church or of the speaker if he is a person in authority, such as a pope. Corresponding to *logos* is the act of God in extending grace to man, which becomes the Christian Logos. This *logos* is characteristically stated or enunciated, not rationally proved, but the message is usually supported by historical examples and by signs, normally in the form of miracles. Finally, corresponding to *pathos* is the use of warnings or promises for the future. The classical orator, of whom Cassiodorus' grandfather may be taken as an example, is a lonely fighter overcoming great odds by rhetorical skill and argumentation. The Christian orator is typically a vessel through which God pours out his grace. In the most extreme form he needs no knowledge, no skill: God provides the words. A description of Gregory the Great as a preacher is an almost perfect expression of the pure Christian tradition:

> The truest mark of the sanctity of the man and what is greatly to be admired is that all his writings show a remarkable unearthly skill, with Christ speaking through him, as we have said. For instance, in his homilies there stands out above all other considerations what He said, "Preach the Gospel to every creature." This he [Gregory], whom God predestined before all ages for our glory, inherited with such full and complete wisdom from Him who is the Wisdom of God shrouded in a mystery that he had his own name among the Roman race, whose fame resounded through all the world—"Golden Voice" because of the sublimely golden charm of his voice. Of that power, the Wisdom of God speaks, saying beautifully, "A treasure to be desired resides in the mouth of wisdom." What was said of Christ may well be applied to him, "Grace is poured into thy lips. . . ."[46]

Between the second and fourth centuries, Christian orators gradually adopted many features of classical rhetoric into the service of the church. This is especially true in the fourth century when Christianity became first legal and then required. The Cappadocian fathers accomplished a remarkable synthesis of classical and Christian rhetoric in their great sermons, paralleling their synthesis of Neoplatonism and Christian theology, while Lactantius and to a greater extent Augustine in *De Doctrina Christiana* sought to combine the two traditions in a theoretical way acceptable to Christian belief. Augustine's great work has had enormous influence over time, but the Christian orator there envisioned surpassed what was feasible for most preachers of the early Middle Ages. When Eugippus made extracts of *De Doctrina Christiana* around 500, he omitted all of Book Four, which is the part relating to rhetoric, and it is hard to show much influence of that book before the Carolingian age. The Second Council of Vaison in 529 sought to encourage preaching: it extended the right to preach from bishops to priests and provided that, if no priest were available, a deacon should read a homily of one of the fathers.[47] Nevertheless, the level of preaching declined in the sixth and seventh centuries. Themes were rarely taken from the Bible, and the lives and passions of the saints became commoner subjects with more immediate meaning to simple congregations.[48] There was a turn to simplicity in all expression, and the basic rhetoric of Christianity reasserted itself over the oratorical preaching of late antiquity. This was of course most true in missionary preaching to the heathen, as seen in the preaching of Boniface, whose success was also heavily dependent on authority—the political support of the Frankish kings and the use of external signs such as chopping down the Hessians' great oak of Thor.[49]

If we turn back to the Tome of King Recared in Toledo, a speech that was doubtless written for him by some Christian bishop, we find that it is better analyzed in terms of Christian than of classical rhetoric. Its rhetorical devices are enunciations of authority as seen in the Bible and in the creeds, of the divine Logos, of God's grace for man, and its pathos comes from God's love and Christian humility. The conversion of Recared from Arianism to orthodoxy is to be followed by the conversion of his people, and that will be accomplished by his authority over them.

Argument from authority has little place in classical rhetoric though classical orators often employed their personal authority when they had any. In the Middle Ages authority plays a major part in all speech situations and especially in the councils and disputes of the church.[50] Here the authority is usually not the personal authority of the speaker but the authorities he cites in support of his position. An excellent example of this kind of rhetoric is furnished by the Synod of Whitby of 664 as described in Bede's *Ecclesiastical History* (3.25). Wilfrid's argument for the orthodox date for Easter is a masterful accumulation of authorities, culminating in that of Saint Peter. Bishop Colman, speaking for the Scots, has only the tradition of his own church and the doubtful authority of Saint John, which Wilfrid easily counters by the argument that John sought temporarily to avoid offending the Jews. King Oswy is persuaded.

Finally we may turn briefly to epideictic, which was under-

[65]

stood in late antiquity and the Middle Ages as the rhetoric of praise or blame (Cassiodorus, *Institutiones* 2.23; Isidore, *Etymologiae* 2.4.5). The chief examples of Latin epideictic oratory from the later empire are the panegyrics of emperors and other public officials. Rules for such compositions are set forth by the third-century Greek rhetorician Menander and touched upon by Emporius and other Latin writers. The major surviving examples are the so-called *Panegyrici Latini*, which consist of Pliny's *Panegyric* of Trajan and eleven similar speeches by senatorial orators delivered in the period between A.D. 289 and 389. There are additional Latin panegyrics from the fourth century by Ausonius and Symmachus, as well as panegyric sermons by Ambrose such as that on the death of Theodosius. Panegyrics in Latin verse begin by the fourth century, those of Claudius Claudianus at the end of the century being the best examples, and continue through the fifth century with examples by Sidonius Apollinaris in Gaul and Dracontius in Africa. The only prose panegyric of the fifth century known to me is one by Flavius Merobaudes, now dated to the early 440s.[51] In the early sixth century there was something of a revival of the form in Ostrogothic Italy, but no examples survive. Verse panegyric of the sixth century is represented best by the writings of Corippus, living under Byzantine rule in Africa,[52] but some features of the form are found in poems of Venantius Fortunatus in France which celebrate, among others, King Chilperic and Queen Fredegunda, whom we met in the trial of Praetextatus. Prose panegyric was closely connected with the ceremonial of the Roman senate or imperial court, and it performed a propaganda function of reasserting imperial and Roman values as well as contributing to a sense of settled social order.[53] These goals were imitated in the panegyrics under the Ostrogoths, but they found no place in the West thereafter. Poets, however, continually found occasion to celebrate their friends or patrons, and many of the commonplaces of panegyric are applied in compositions throughout the Middle Ages. Curtius has traced some of the history of such composition.[54] The conventions of Latin panegyric poetry were not, however, learned from the study of rhetorical theory but from imitation of earlier poetic examples.

Epideictic passages are frequently inserted in other forms of classical speech, as by Cicero when he praises Pompey in his deliberative oration for the Manilian law, and there were doubtless many occasions in the early Middle Ages when courtiers or supplicants flattered or fawned upon the powerful or inveighed against their enemies with the ultimate goal of obtaining some decision in their own behalf. The written form corresponding to this would be passages of praise or blame inserted in letters in both ancient and medieval times. Even Gregory the Great carefully praises rulers when he writes to them. The one situation in early Medieval Latin in which we can see evidence for praise for the sake of praise comes in the celebration of God and of the saints. Victricius' praise of the saints in connection with the arrival of relics in the fourth century[55] and the poem of Dracontius *On the Praises of God* in the fifth century are early examples of a purely Christian kind of epideictic. More literary saints' lives from late antiquity often show the specific influence of classical panegyric, but such lives, like sermons, tended to become simpler as time passed, less classical, more Christian.[56] Oral celebration of God and the saints also existed in preaching in the early Middle Ages. Here we have a characteristic early medieval epideictic form, in so far as the intention was purely praise in which the congregation might join. But the more strongly the preacher dwelt upon the message that his congregation should go out into the world and imitate the saints, the more the form is one of deliberative rhetoric that calls for future action in the congregation's best interests.

One of the finest pieces of epideictic speech from the early Middle Ages is the address *In Praise of the Church* by Leander, elder brother of Isidore of Seville, delivered at the end of the Third Council of Toledo in 589 and preserved like the speech of King Recared among the acts of that council.[57] It is labelled a "homily" in the texts, which is perhaps consistent with the usage of the times and could be justified by the fact that it contains exegesis of some passages of Scripture, but it is in fact a triumphant celebration of the victory of catholic Christianity over Arianism in Spain. All the credit is given to God and the church; not one word is said about King Recared. Thus the structure is quite unlike that of classical panegyric, which usually proceeds chronologically or topically through the career of the hero being celebrated. The language is good, largely classical, Latin, arranged in beautifully balanced sentences, adorned with classical figures of speech and dignified by accentual rhythms. The amplification of the basically simple thought is worthy of any Roman panegyrist. It is accomplished not by the *loci* of classical rhetoric but by devices of Christian rhetoric—quotations from the Bible, allegorical exegesis, and such biblical imagery as the lilies and thorns of the field, Christ the bridegroom, and the like. The topic of authority also appears. At one point Leander says: *hoc non coniecturae sensus nostri sed scripturae divinae auctoriate probetur*, a classical chiasmus that might be paraphrased, "This is proved not by the devices of classical rhetoric, but by the divine Scripture's authority."[58]

In conclusion, there are in the Latin speech of the early Middle Ages at least three distinct rhetorics to be found occurring in various combinations and conflicts. The only one existing in fully conceptualized form is the classical tradition as expounded by Cassiodorus, Isidore, or Alcuin. In practice it is best seen in trials before ecclesiastic courts but, even there, rarely in a pure form. A second rhetoric is the Christian tradition of the Bible, which was applied by the earlier fathers of the church, imitated by preachers before humble audiences, and widely utilized on public religious occasions of speech. Although this tradition is partially conceptualized by Augustine, his synthesis is deeply imbued with classical forms and did not ideally meet the needs of the pre-Carolingian age. The third rhetoric might be called Germanic, though it is characteristic of any brutal time; it is the rhetoric of the direct application of authority, of trial by ordeal, of intimidation, and of force. In the influential prologue to *De Inventione*, Cicero had spoken of such rhetoric solely as anterior to the development of classical forms, but it lay dormant and presented itself when conditions were right. In addition to Latin rhetorics there existed in the early Middle Ages some vernacular rhetorics with distinctive features; the Irish "retoric" is perhaps the most remarkable. Much more, in my judgment, could be learned about the interworkings of these rhetorics, even from the scanty records at our disposal. Study of medieval rhetoric, and that of the Renaissance as well, has been inhibited by easy identification of it with not only ornaments of style, versification, and poetic topics but with the distinctive features of classical rhetoric as a whole—to the neglect of other rhetorical traditions.

NOTES

1. I am indebted for bibliographical assistance in the preparation of this paper to two graduate students at the University of North Carolina, Hannah C. Thomas and Elizabeth E. Zakarison. For further discussion of the conceptualization of rhetoric and of the relationship between oral and literary rhetoric, see George A. Kennedy, *Classical Rhetoric and Its Christian and Secular Tradition* (Chapel Hill: University of North Carolina Press, 1980), chs. I and VI.

2. See James Westfall Thompson, *The Literacy of the Laity in the Middle Ages*, University of California Publications in Education, 9 (Berkeley: University of California Press, 1939), pp. 1–26.

3. See *European Literature and the Latin Middle Ages* (Princeton: Princeton University Press, 1967), p. 69.

4. There are two separate traditions: one, following Martianus Capella, put rhetoric after dialectic and is seen in Gregory of Tours 10.31; the other and commoner tradition put rhetoric between grammar and dialectic. This represents ancient practice and was given definitive statement by Cassiodorus and Isidore, but both traditions are found in the later Middle Ages.

5. See the overall treatment of the subject in James J. Murphy, *Rhetoric in the Middle Ages: A History of Rhetorical Theory from Saint Augustine to the Renaissance* (Berkeley: University of California Press, 1974).

6. See John O. Ward, "*Artificiosa Eloquentia* in the Middle Ages," Ph.D. dissertation, University of Toronto, 1972 (National Library of Canada, *Canadian Theses on Microfilm*, 13083), and his article "From Antiquity to the Renaissance: Glosses and Commentaries on Cicero's *Rhetorica*," in James J. Murphy, editor, *Medieval Eloquence: Studies in the Theory and Practice of Medieval Rhetoric* (Berkeley: University of California Press, 1978), pp. 25–67.

7. How the identification of rhetoric and metrics developed may be seen from the fifth-century work of Rufinus of Antioch, *Litteratoris de Compositione et de Metris Oratorum*: text in Heinrich Keil, editor, *Grammatici Latini*, 6 (Leipzig: Teubner, 1874), pp. 561–78; translated by Ian Thomson in Joseph M. Miller, Michael H. Prosser, and Thomas W. Benson, editors, *Readings in Medieval Rhetoric* (Bloomington: University of Indiana Press,

1973), pp. 37–51. On early medieval identification of rhetoric and metrics see Ward, "*Artificiosa Eloquentia*," pp. 116–17.

8. See Terrot Reavely Glover, *Life and Letters in the Fourth Century* (Cambridge: Cambridge University Press, 1901); Theodore Haarhoff, *Schools of Gaul: A Study of Pagan and Christian Education in the Last Century of the Western Empire* (Oxford: Oxford University Press, 1920); Nora K. Chadwick, *Poetry and Letters in Early Christian Gaul* (London: Bowes and Bowes, 1955); and especially Pierre Riché, *Education and Culture in the Barbarian West, Sixth through Eighth Centuries*, translated by John J. Contreni (Columbia: University of South Carolina Press, 1976), pp. 21–51.

9. See *Confessions* 5.13.23; H. I. Marrou, *A History of Education in Antiquity*, translated by George Lamb (New York: Sheed and Ward, 1956), pp. 400–418, and Riché, *Education and Culture*, p. 7.

10. See H. I. Marrou, "Autour de la bibliothèque du pape Agapit," *Mélanges d'Archéologie et d'Histoire* 48 (1931): 157–65; and *History of Education*, p. 579.

11. See *Corpus Juris Civilis*, Novellae, App. VII, 22, as edited by Rudolf Schöll (Berlin: Weidmann, 1912), p. 802; and Riché, *Education and Culture*, p. 140.

12. See Riché, *Education and Culture*, pp. 404–15.

13. See Jacques Fontaine, *Isidore de Seville et la culture classique dans l'Espagne wisigothique* (Paris: Etudes Augustiniennes, 1959), pp. 223–24.

14. See Johannes Sundwall, *Abhandlungen zur Geschichte des ausgehenden Römertums* (Helsinki: Centraltryckeri och Bokbinderi Aktiebolag, 1919), pp. 1–83; and Riché, *Education and Culture*, pp. 24–27.

15. See Fontaine, *Isidore de Seville*, p. 241; and *Paulys Real-Encyclopädie der classischen Altertumswissenschaft*, 5 (Stuttgart, 1905), col. 2535.

16. See Curtius, *European Literature*, p. 159.

17. See Fontaine, *Isidore de Seville*, p. 261.

18. See Riché, *Education and Culture*, p. 35.

19. See Ward, "*Artificiosa Eloquentia*," pp. 178 and 184–91. Basic reference is Richer, *Historia Francorum* 3.48.

20. See Leslie Weber Jones, *An Introduction to Divine and Human Readings by Cassiodorus Senator* (New York: Columbia University Press, 1946), p. 67. For the text see *Cassiodori Senatoris Institutiones*, edited by R. A. B. Mynors (Oxford: Oxford University Press, 1937). On Cassiodorus' life and works, see James J. O'Donnell, *Cassiodorus* (Berkeley: University of California Press, 1979).

21. See Ursula Hahner, *Cassiodors Psalmenkommentar: Sprachliche Untersuchungen* (Munich: Arbeo Gesellschaft, 1973); and Reinhard Schliebem, *Christliche Theologie und Philologie in der Spätantike: Die schulwissenschaftlichen Methoden der Psalmenexegese Cassiodors* (Berlin: de Gruyter, 1974).

22. Fontaine, *Isidore de Seville*, p. 224, attributes the omission of discus-

sion of style to "méfiance à l'égard de ces complaisances vaines." This seems unlikely considering Cassiodorus' references to figures elsewhere in the *Institutes* and in the *Commentary on the Psalms*. It should be noted that some other late antique works on rhetoric also omit style, for example the Pseudo-Augustine *De Rhetorica*, and that Cicero's *De Inventione* was more popular than *Rhetorica ad Herennium*, even though the former omits style and the latter includes it.

23. See Jones, *Introduction*, p. 150. In our texts the passage is Psalm 36:5–6.

24. See Jones, *Introduction*, pp. 151–52. The reference is to the *Commentary on the Psalms*, ch. 31.

25. See Jones, *Introduction*, pp. 157–58.

26. See ibid., p. 150.

27. See Katherine Fischer Drew, *The Lombard Laws* (Philadelphia: University of Pennsylvania Press, 1973), pp. 25–28.

28. See 2.13; 5.8; 6.17. Examples of "trials" are 4.47 and 6.29.

29. For a general account of law and procedure see Samuel Dill, *Roman Society in Gaul in the Merovingian Age* (London: Macmillan, 1926), pp. 40–76.

30. See Harriet Pratt Lattin, *The Letters of Gerbert, with His Papal Privileges as Sylvester II* (New York: Columbia University Press, 1961), pp. 236–62.

31. For text, German translation, and some notes see the edition of Rudolf Buchner, *Gregorii Episcopi Turonensis Historiarum Libri Decem*, 2 vols. (Darmstadt: Wissenschaftliche Buchgessellschaft, 1970). The chapter can be found in English in Ernest Brehaut, *History of the Franks by Gregory of Tours: Selections Translated with Notes* (New York: W. W. Norton, 1969), pp. 119–25.

32. Gregory, 7.16, says there were forty-five bishops in the council, though Buchner, *Gregorii Episcopi*, 2:111, questions the number.

33. See Jones, *Introduction*, p. 155.

34. There is also a broth of chicken and chickpeas (Buchner, *Gregorii Episcopi*, 1:314, lines 27–29), but what Gregory ultimately takes is *panis et vinum* (p. 316, lines 1–2).

35. Riché, *Education and Culture*, suggests that they were hymns.

36. See Leslie W. Jones, "The Influence of Cassiodorus on Medieval Culture," *Speculum* 20 (1945): 433–42. Similarities between Cassiodorus and the account of rhetoric in Alcuin exist but may have come through Isidore; see Wilbur Samuel Howell, *The Rhetoric of Alcuin and Charlemagne* (Princeton: Princeton University Press, 1941), pp. 23 and 159–60. Cassiodorus' *Institutes*, though known to Isidore in Spain, was probably not known to Gregory the Great in Rome around 600; see Riché, *Education and Culture*, p. 153.

[71]

37. See *Acta Sanctorum*, 1 (Paris and Rome: Bollandist Society, 1866), p. 53.

38. See P. D. King, *Law and Society in the Visigothic Kingdom* (Cambridge: Cambridge University Press, 1972), especially pp. 101–21.

39. See Fontaine, *Isidore de Seville*, pp. 334–35.

40. See Luitpold Wallach, *Alcuin and Charlemagne: Studies in Carolingian History and Literature*, Cornell Studies in Classical Philology, 32 (Ithaca: Cornell University Press, 1959), pp. 73–82.

41. See Ward, "*Artificiosa Eloquentia*," p. 126.

42. See Johannes Sundwall, "Der Senat und die Politik," *Abhandlungen*, pp. 178–308.

43. See Thomas Hodgkin, *The Letters of Cassiodorus* (London: Henry Frowde, 1886), p. 146.

44. The text and Spanish translation in José Vives, *Concilios Visigóticos e Hispano-Romanos* (Madrid: Consejo superior de investigaciones científicas, 1963), pp. 107–17. For translation see J. N. Hillgarth, editor, *The Conversion of Western Europe, 300–750* (Englewood Cliffs, N.J.: Prentice-Hall, 1969), pp. 85–89.

45. *Classical Rhetoric*, ch. 7; *New Testament Interpretation through Rhetorical Criticism* (Chapel Hill: University of North Carolina Press, 1984).

46. From *The Oldest Life of Pope St. Gregory*, by A Monk of Whitby, ch. 24, in Charles W. Jones, *Saints' Lives and Chronicles in Early England* (Ithaca: Cornell University Press, 1947), pp. 112–13.

47. See *Concilia Galliae A. 511–A. 695*, edited by Carlo de Clerq (Turnholti: Brepols, 1963), pp. 78–79.

48. See Riché, *Education and Culture*, pp. 91–95.

49. See Donald Andreini, "The Confrontation of Missionary and Pagan in the Early Middle Ages: A Study of Missionary Methods and Ideas, and the Response of the Pagans c. 595–814," Ph.D. dissertation, Brandeis University, 1969 (*Dissertation Abstracts* 31 [1970]: 327A) and J. N. Hillgarth, ed., *Conversion of Western Europe, 300–750* (Englewood Cliffs, N.J.: Prentice-Hall, 1969). On Boniface and the oak see George W. Robinson, *The Life of Saint Boniface by Willibald* (Cambridge: Harvard University Press, 1916), pp. 63–64.

50. See Karl F. Morrison, *Tradition and Authority in the Western Church, 300–1140* (Princeton: Princeton University Press, 1969), especially pp. 111–52.

51. See Frank M. Clover, "Flavius Merobaudes: A Translation and Historical Commentary," *Transactions of the American Philosophical Society* 61.1 (1971): 38.

52. See Averil Cameron, *Flavius Cresconius Corippus In Laudem Justini Augusti Minoris* (London: Athlone Press, 1976), pp. 1–14.

53. See Sabine MacCormack, "Latin Prose Panegyrics: Tradition and

Discontinuity in the Later Roman Empire," *Revue des études augustiniennes* 22 (1976): 29–77.

54. *European Literature*, pp. 154–202.

55. See Hillgarth, ed. *Conversion of Western Europe*, pp. 22–27.

56. See Riché, *Education and Culture*, pp. 272–73, with additional bibliography.

57. For the text with Spanish translation see Vives, *Concilios visigóticos*, pp. 139–44.

58. Ibid., p. 34, lines 9–11.

IV

Pure and Impure Pastoral

Louis L. Martz
Yale University

My title is adapted from an essay by Robert Penn Warren, "Pure and Impure Poetry," a classic essay of the Old New Criticism in which the principles of that still-surviving mode of literary study are set forth in clear, creative terms. Warren believes that the search for a pure essence of poetry is an illusion. Poetry, he says, may be pure, as a concept, but in actual existence, poems are never pure—or if they are, they are weak, attenuated things, devoid of the sustenance of poetical life, which lies in meeting and dealing with "recalcitrant elements," "resistances." Poetry, according to this view, "does not inhere in any particular element but depends upon the set of relationships, the structure, which we call the poem." Hence a poem, "to be good," becomes "a motion toward a point of rest, but if it is not a resisted motion, it is motion of no consequence."[1]

Now I notice, in reading various studies of pastoral, that critics tend to seek out what they call "pure pastoral," or "true pastoral," or sometimes they place "pastoral" in quotation marks, as though it were an unattainable ideal not purely present in any significant pastoral action. Pastoral longs to be pure; it struggles to shake off impurities, the grit and dust and sweat of daily being; but it is seldom found in all its longed-for purity. When it is, we seem to find it in a song, a pastoral moment supported by real or imagined music, as in this lyric by Milton for which we have the music by Henry Lawes:

> Sweet Echo, sweetest Nymph that liv'st unseen
> Within thy airy shell
> By slow *Meander's* margent green,

And in the violet-imbroider'd vale
   Where the love-lorn Nightingale
Nightly to thee her sad Song mourneth well.
Canst thou not tell me of a gentle Pair
   That likest thy *Narcissus* are?
      O if thou have
   Hid them in som flowry Cave,
     Tell me but where
Sweet Queen of Parly, Daughter of the Sphear,
So maist thou be translated to the skies,
And give resounding grace to all Heav'ns Harmonies.[2]

There are no shepherds here, though a spirit attired as a shepherd is not far off; yet this song from *Comus* mingles nature's beauty with the music of the spheres to create a moment of peace that could be called "pastoral." But is its harmony pure? These Ovidian myths of Echo, Narcissus, and Philomela are sad and painful tales of the ravages of human passion. In Ovid a peaceful pool, surrounded by grass and shaded by trees, is shattered by the self-love of Narcissus; and we know the horrors for which the nightingale "her sad Song mourneth well."[3] Philomela suffered her violation in the depths of a dark wood such as that in which the Lady in *Comus* is now singing, just before she falls into the snare of a tempter disguised as a shepherd. Disaster in a wood is a favorite motif in Ovid's *Metamorphoses*, as in the episode where Circe transforms Picus because he remains faithful to the singer Canens.[4] The struggle to rescue pure pastoral from the threat of an Ovidian myth lies at the heart of Milton's *Comus*.

Take a song that exists by itself in the famous Elizabethan anthology of pastoral poetry, *Englands Helicon* (1600), a song attributed to Nicholas Breton, and this time a song that directly involves shepherds. The speaker in this poem overhears a conversation between Phillida and Coridon as he walks "by the Wood side" in "the merry moneth of May:"

Much a-doo there was God wot,
He would loue, and she would not.
She sayd neuer man was true,

He sayd, none was false to you.
He sayd, he had lou'd her long,
She sayd, Loue should haue no wrong.
Coridon would kisse her then,
She said, Maides must kisse no men,
Till they did for good and all.
Then she made the Sheepheard call
All the heauens to witnesse truth:
Neuer lou'd a truer youth.
Thus with many a pretty oath,
Yea and nay, and faith and troth,
Such as silly Sheepheards vse,
When they will not Loue abuse;
Loue, which had beene long deluded,
Was with kisses sweete concluded.
And *Phillida* with garlands gay:
Was made the Lady of the May.[5]

Pure pastoral? Yes, and yet we note certain resistances that give the poem its fragile charm: the insistent doubt of men's truth in Phillida's mind; and the narrator's comment that such vows of faith and troth live in the world of "silly Sheepheards," simple, naive rustics—far from the sophistications and deceptions that this commentator evidently knows. This song, in fact, was not designed to stand by itself; it was part of *The Honorable Entertainement gieuen to the Queenes Maiestie in Progresse, at Eluetham in Hampshire, by the right Honorable the Earle of Hertford* in 1591—the sort of entertainment that saved the queen money, while bankrupting her unfortunate hosts. "On Wednesday morning, about nine of the clock," we read: "as her Maiestie opened a casement of her gallerie window, ther were three excellent Musitians, who being disguised in auncient countrey attire, did greet her with a pleasant song of Coridon and Phyllida, made in three parts of purpose. The song, as well for the worth of the Dittie, as for the aptnes of the note thereto applied, it pleased her Highnesse, after it had beene once sung, to command it againe, and highly to grace it

[76]

with her chearefull acceptance and commendation."[6] Such pastoral charms live best, it seems, in the context of courtly sophistication.

The editor of *Englands Helicon* has indeed attempted to create a book of pure pastorals by extracting many of his poems from their often recalcitrant contexts in Sidney's *Astrophil and Stella* or *Arcadia*, Greene's *Menaphon*, Spenser's *Shepheardes Calender*, Lodge's *Rosalynde*, Bartholomew Yong's translation of Montemayor's *Diana*, and other romances, entertainments, and poetical sequences of the time. Such a procedure is quite in line with the vision of pure pastoral implied in the verses from Tibullus (II.i.13–14) that appear on the title page of the first edition of this collection: "Casta placent superis, pura cum veste venite, / Et manibus puris sumite fontis aquam." ("Chaste things please the gods: come with pure garments and with clean hands take up the water of the spring.") In *Englands Helicon* the poems, thus cleansed, frequently seem bland and inert, for they have lost their context of resistance.

These, however, are late uses of pastoral; the pure stream, perhaps, has been polluted over the centuries. If we go back to the antique examples, in Theocritus and Vergil, can we not find an aboriginal purity? In places, yes. The opening of the first idyll of Theocritus presents the archetypal setting for all pastoral, as Thyrsis the shepherd and the unnamed goatherd converse: "Sweet music, goatherd," says Thyrsis, "the pine by the spring yonder / makes with its whispering: sweet, too, your fluting, / and worthy to win second prize after Pan."[7] The goatherd replies: "Sweeter, shepherd, your song than the gushing / water that pours from the high rock yonder." Then Thyrsis asks:

> I pray by the nymphs, goatherd, will you sit
> on the slope of the hillock, there by the tamarisks,
> and play on your pipe, while I mind your goats?

Music of man in harmony with nature's music: this is pure pastoral, yes, but the harmony is fragile. For the goatherd replies to this request for piping:

[77]

Shepherd, I may not, for reverence of Pan,
pipe in the noonday; at that hour he rests,
worn out with the hunt. He is wrathful if roused . . .

No wonder Pan always wins the first prize. "But you, Thyrsis,
sing the sorrows of Daphnis, / and have brought to perfection the
bucolic art"; sing your song, he says, "under this elm tree." As a
reward, along with milk from his goats, he offers the famous "ivy-
wood bowl," delicately carved with ivy and acanthus around the
borders and showing three inset scenes. One presents two lovers
competing unsuccessfully for the love of a laughing maiden:
"Love has drawn circles under their eyes; they labor in vain."
Along with this "an old fisherman is depicted" standing on a rock,
laboring to drag his net, "the picture of toil." Finally we have a
complex picture of a small boy who is supposed to be guarding a
vineyard from the foxes, but he is so busy weaving a cage for
locusts that he does not notice one fox eating the grapes and another approaching to steal his lunch from his bag. The sorrows,
labors, and misfortunes of daily life, then, are not to be excluded
from pastoral, but they are carved within delicate, yet firm, borders of ivy and acanthus, symbols of poetical and artistic inspiration. Pastoral art defines a limit, a perspective, a distancing, that
diminishes the pain, while recognizing its necessity.

Come, says the goatherd, begin your song of Daphnis: "Pointless to keep music in store / till Hades bring all to blank oblivion."
Pastoral art, then, lives with the presence of death, as now in
Thyrsis' great lament for Daphnis, the tragedy of an ancient legend of faith and infidelity in love is woven into a harmony controlled, limited, by the refrain, repeated with a slight variation
fifteen times: "Begin the bucolic theme, kind Muses, begin. . . .
Begin the bucolic theme: Muses, begin again." Then at the climax
of the lament, as Daphnis calls upon Pan, the refrain changes to
"Break the bucolic theme; break it off, Muses," four times repeated, as Daphnis dies. The singer holds the sorrow within the
firm bordering of art, and the whole idyll ends with a realistic note
characteristic of Theocritus: "Come here, Kissaitha," the goatherd
calls to the she-goat; "You milk her," he says to Thyrsis. Now

"stop prancing about," he calls to the other she-goats, or billy goat will be after you. Here is yet another mode of control, limit; the idyll has returned from legend to the earth we know.

Consider next another famous moment of pure pastoral from the antique past:

Fortunate senex! You will stay here, between the rivers that you know so well, by springs that have their Nymphs, and find some cool spot underneath the trees. Time and again, as it has always done, the hedge there, leading from your neighbour's land, will have its willow-blossom rifled by Hyblaean bees and coax you with a gentle humming through the gates of sleep. On the other side, at the foot of the high rock, you will have the vine-dresser singing to the breezes; while all the time your dear full-throated pigeons will be heard, and the turtle-dove high in the elm will never bring her cooing to an end.[8]

These lines are spoken by a dispossessed and despairing man, the goatherd Meliboeus in Vergil's first eclogue. His land has been given to a soldier and now he is forced to drive his goats into a painful exile. In those famous lines, the essence of pure pastoral, he is lamenting the happy life now lost to him, but preserved for his friend Tityrus through the power of a great man in Rome. The idealized quality of his pastoral vision here is recognized by Meliboeus even before he sings it, as he says that the really fortunate thing for Tityrus lies in the fact that his friend still possesses his own land, poor as it is. "And it's enough for you, even though the bare rock and the marshland with its mud and reeds encroach on all your pastures." *Et tibi magna satis*: "it's big enough for you." Its ideal qualities lie in the mind of the exiled observer. All pastoral poetry might thus be seen as poetry of exile.

What shall we say of the even more extravagantly idealized vision in Vergil's fourth eclogue, the Messianic eclogue, in which Vergil foresees the return of the Golden Age at the birth of a miraculous child? A vast body of portentous interpretation has been lavished upon this poem for nearly two thousand years, but I am encouraged by the views of William Berg[9] to admit my misgivings about finding such solemn meanings in the eclogue. Such interpretations seem to burst the bounds of pastoral, whereas in his other eclogues Vergil holds the visions of pure pastoral within firm control. Vergil is well aware that in this vision he is stretching the limits of pastoral at least to the breaking point, for in his opening he says: "Sicelides Musae, paulo maiora canamus [Muses of Sicily, let us attempt a rather more exalted theme]." One should stress the *paulo maiora*: somewhat greater, a little bit greater, not vastly so, not utterly beyond the sylvan scene. How then can the hyperbole be controlled? Perhaps the clue lies in a quiet sense of humor that seems to run throughout, with an implication that his talented friend Pollio—consul, poet, and friend of Catullus—will understand the complex tone of recognized impossibility. "Under your leadership all traces that remain of our iniquity will be effaced and, as they vanish, free the world from its long night of horror." This is what we all wish for our children—those children who are all, at their births, miracles—may their births usher in a new age in which they will not have to undergo the sufferings of their parents. The new-born child, whoever the child is (Pollio's, Antony's, Octavian's), deserves the tribute of the pastoral vision in its full purity: "No mattock will molest the soil, no pruning-knife the vine; and then at last the sturdy plowman will free his oxen from the yoke. Wool will be taught no more to cheat the eye with this tint or with that, but the ram himself in his own meadows will change the colour of his fleece, now to the soft glow of a purple dye, now to a saffron yellow. Lambs at their pastures will find themselves in scarlet coats."

Is there not a quiet, teasing humor here, a complex subtle tone such as only Vergil can achieve? We can understand why, over the ages, portentous interpretations have been inevitable, and yet perhaps a sad Vergilian smile should warn us not to take this fantasy so solemnly. Vergil's ending seems to bear out this reading of the subtle tone:

incipe, parve puer, risu cognoscere matrem
(matri longa decem tulerunt fastidia menses)
incipe, parve puer: qui non risere parenti,[10]
nec deus hunc mensa, dea nec dignata cubili est.

Begin, then, little boy, to greet your mother with a
smile: the ten long months have left her sick at

heart. Begin, little boy: no one who has not
given his mother a smile has ever been thought worthy
of his table by a god, or by a goddess of her bed.

Is this the tone of a Sybilline utterance? Everywhere we turn in
Vergil's eclogues we may feel him testing the limits of pastoral
action: how far can one go in pursuit of the ideal without provok-
ing the anger and revenge of those recalcitrant elements (such as
Pan) that demand a limit, require a reverence for the facts of human existence? In the second eclogue the shepherd Corydon, in a
frenzy of frustrated love, breaks the pastoral harmony into *incon-
dita* ("disordered shreds of song") until an underlying grasp on
reality emerges firmly at the close and recognizes the need for a
limit: "Me tamen urit amor: quis enim modus adsit amori?" "But
love is burning me up": what measure, what rule, what limit can
one set for love? *Modus* is the clue to successful pastoral action.
And the answer immediately follows as the shepherd says to himself: "Corydon, Corydon, what is this madness that has got you
down? You have left your vines half-pruned and the elms they
grow on thick with leaves. Rather than this, why not get busy on a
useful piece of work and plait a basket with some osier-twigs or
pliant reeds? If this Alexis treats you with contempt, you'll find
another."

So in the third eclogue Palaemon, judge of the singing contest,
gives us the pastoral ideal at the center, almost the mathematical
center of the poem—fifty-four lines precede this vision, and fifty-
two lines follow: "Sing on, then, since we are seated on soft grass,
and the year is at its loveliest, with growing crops in every field,
fruit coming on every tree, and all the woods in leaf. Damoetas,
you will lead off, and Menalcas follow, replying to you every time.
Alternate song is what the Muses love."

The fifty-four lines preceding this passage contain a humorous
slanging match between Menalcas and Damoetas, as they hurl
clever insults at each other, summing up in good humor all the
destructive impulses in mankind. We note that the alternating
passages here do not match in length; they vary from four lines
to three, two, four, five, four, three, four. Then they turn to de-

scribe two beautiful pairs of carved wooden cups (inherited from Theocritus) that are embossed with ivy and acanthus and include carved figures representing mathematical and musical control: two of them are sages who "mapped the whole celestial sphere" and another is Orpheus himself. After this Palaemon's lines create the pastoral center, and from here all turns to measure, carefully controlled in alternating couplets. These are so skillfully matched that, although they contain memories of wolves, "Amaryllis's angry moods," Bavius's rotten verses, the snake in the grass, the risky river bank, and love afflicting both the herd and the herdsman, none of these impurities can break or shake the steady equilibrium of alternate song so loved by the Muses and so measured that Palaemon is unable to choose between the two singers and awards a prize heifer to both.

It is this *modus*, this measure, this equilibrium of forces that Vergil is constantly testing, pressing outward to include themes that lie far beyond the pastoral center. Thus, in the sixth eclogue, Vergil admits at the outset that at times "kings and battles filled my thoughts," but he declines to sing "the unhappy chronicles of war" even though their existence must be recognized by the pastoral singer. Instead he turns to test the limits of pastoral by giving us the song of Silenus, which tells the grand story of the creation of the universe and also, at greater length, of Pasiphae's desperate passion for the snow-white bull, whose pastoral existence ironically evades her grasp: "Meanwhile your lover rests his snow-white flank on a soft bed of hyacinths, chewing the pale grass under a dark ilex-tree, or else pursues one of the many heifers of the herd." Silenus mentions other tales of suffering and transformation, such as the tales of Scylla and Philomela. Here, then, is the eclogue that, as everyone points out, foreshadows and perhaps inspired Ovid's great epic of *furor* and *amor*, but we should note the inversion of pastoral values involved in Ovid's *Metamorphoses*. Vergil, though his song of Silenus ranges far and wide, holds all firmly within the pastoral setting, but Ovid adapts the pastoral setting of peaceful pools, springs, caves, and woods to make them into places of deceptive peace—where Callisto is attacked by Jove, Hermaphroditus is enticed by Salmacis, the passion of Alpheus is aroused by Arethusa, and Diana is glimpsed while bathing by the unfortunate Actaeon.[11] Ovid's *Metamorphoses* reveal, often with cruel detail, the furious forces that underlie such pastoral glimpses, but Vergil's eclogues recognize the forces of disorder from a distance, from beneath the shade of the beech tree, the ilex, or the elm. "How safe, methinks, and strong, behind / These trees have I encamped my mind," in Andrew Marvell's words. Thus the unruly Eclogue 6, with its song of Silenus, is held in place by being embraced on the one side, in Eclogue 5, by the vision of Daphnis who is immortalized as god of singing shepherds, while on the other side, in Eclogue 7, we find a match of alternate song by Corydon and Thyrsis, with Daphnis presiding as a benevolent presence.

Yet in the opening of the eighth eclogue Vergil again shows his longing to burst the measure of pastoral as he longs to celebrate the achievement of a friend who has achieved greatness both as a military leader and as a composer of tragedies: "Ah, will the day ever come when I shall be allowed to chronicle your deeds? Will the day come when I can celebrate your tragedies, sole rivals of the Muse of Sophocles, through all the world? My first notes were inspired by you: for you my last will sound. Accept this poem, begun at your command, and let its ivy twine with the victor's laurels round your brow."

Then he proceeds to present two songs of love, one unhappy, one fulfilled, but both controlled by firmly repeated refrains: "Reed-pipe of Maenalus, support me in my song;" "Bring Daphnis from the town, my spells, bring Daphnis home." In Eclogue 9 we return to the threat of dispossession, as Lycidas meets Moeris driving his flocks along the road to town: "Oh, Lycidas, a blow has fallen on us—one we never even feared. That I should live to see a total stranger seize our farm and say, 'This is my property: be off!'—to us who have always worked the land! Now, we are a miserable, beaten crew; and, as would happen in this topsy-turvy world, it is for him that I'm taking in these kids—bad luck go with them!"

Lycidas, whose name comes from the goatherd-poet in the seventh idyll of Theocritus, represents the spirit of poetry; he says he has heard that the land was saved "by your dear Menalcas and his poetry." Not so, not so, says the old and dispirited Moeris, poetry has no such power. Yet they both go on to remember and sing certain fragments of Menalcas's poetry, though Moeris laments that his memory is failing and that he is even losing his voice. Lycidas, a young poet, also has some trouble recalling the words of Menalcas, but this, no doubt, is because he has not heard them as often as Moeris. Certainly Lycidas does not share the gloom of old Moeris; he still has confidence that poetry will prevail and urges his companion to "go forward singing all the way." I cannot share the pessimistic interpretation that Putnam has given to this poem.[12] Moeris speaks the discouragement of age, Lycidas the hopefulness of youth; the points of view seem well-balanced throughout the poem, until at the very end the balance tips toward the side of Lycidas, for Moeris concedes that Menalcas will live to recite his redeeming art: "Menalcas will recite these poems to you to your heart's content"; and "As for Menalcas' songs, we shall sing them all the better when he comes to us himself."

Finally, in Eclogue 10, summation of the whole, Vergil comes to grips with two irremediable enemies of the pastoral center: military struggle, and, worst of all, the desperate, raging, unsatisfied love of the Latin elegiac poets, both represented in the figure of his friend Gallus. "Begin," Vergil says to his pastoral muse Arethusa, "and may your stream slide under the Sicilian waves unmingled with the harsh sea-brine," but this prayer for pure pastoral cannot be answered. The madness of Gallus's love for Lycoris, who has run off to the North with a soldier, cannot be tempered, nor can his other *insanus amor*, his mad love for the stern god of war. Though all the pastoral deities come to plead with him—Apollo, Silvanus, Pan himself—Gallus can find no comfort, no *modus*, in pastoral song: "No, all is over. Tree-nymphs and poetry itself have ceased to please. Even you have failed, woodlands; away with you! . . . Love carries all before him: I too must yield to Love." It is the very theme of Ovid's *Metamorphoses*: there are aspects of human passion that pastoral cannot limit or redeem. Gallus is lost, and the pastoral voice can only contemplate his tragedy and soothe its memories with sad affection: "Pierian god-

[84]

desses, let these lines suffice for your poet to have sung, as he sat and wove a basket with slim marsh-mallow twigs. I count on you to make the most of them to Gallus—Gallus, my love for whom grows as much hour by hour as the green alder shoots up when the spring is young."

Vergil, then, has brought into his eclogues every impurity that can threaten the pastoral center; but the pastoral attitude, the pastoral *modus*, holds the woes of mankind within its purifying, tempering vision.

So it is with all great pastoral works of later years. At the pastoral heart of Spenser's sixth book of the *Faerie Queene*, the vision of Colin Clout brings, for a moment, a dance of harmony within the turbulent world, just as in his *Shepheardes Calender* the steady, accepted movement of the months controls and enfolds the varied worlds of love and court and church that threaten constantly to erode and destroy the pastoral vision. So too, in that ancient work that provided Spenser with more than his title: *The Kalender of Shepherdes*, that old almanac filled with woodcuts and containing, as the translator of 1508 says, "many wonderful matters both poetical, philosophical, and theological."[13] This book appeared in France late in the fifteenth century and went through many, many, constantly revised editions, both in England and in France, up through the middle of the seventeenth century. It includes calendars for the feasts of the church, schedules for computing the movement of the constellations, advice on how to avoid vices and achieve virtues, along with a great deal of doggerel verse scattered throughout. The French title is indeed appropriate: *Le Compost et Kalendrier des Bergiers*. *Compost*: the word comes into the English versions too, not in the title, but in the text, which says, "This present boke is namyd the compot for it comprehendis fully all the compot and more for the dayes, owers, and momentis and the newe mones and the clyppys of the sonne and the mone and of the synes that the mone is in euery daye. And this boke was made for them that be no clarkes, to brynge them to greate vnderstondynge."[14]

Oskar Sommer, the editor of the 1892 edition of this *Kalender*, defines *compot* as "compost, composition, or mixture,"[15] but this is, strictly speaking, wrong. As the English spelling indicates, *compot* is derived from Latin *computus* and means calculation, computation, way of reckoning—for feasts of the church, movements of the stars, and so on. Through some confusion with the Latin *compositum*, the French long since had put the *s* in the word, thus confusing the two meanings: computation and mixture of miscellaneous stuff. No one could blame those readers who were not "clarkes" if they took the word to refer to their own compost heaps. In any case, the figure who presides over this compost or compot is the wise shepherd frequently referred to throughout as the purveyor of wisdom, especially the "master shepherd" who opens the book with an account of the months of the year described by analogy with the life of man:

> Than cometh Maye that is fayre & plesaunt / than byrdes syngeth in the foreste nyght and day, the sonne shynethe hote, and as than is man moste ioly & plesaunt and of delyuer [active, agile] strengthe & seketh playes & sportes for than is he therty yere. Than cometh Iune & than is the sonne hyest in his meridyornall. He maye assende no hyeer in his stacyone. His glemerrynge goldene beames rypethe the corne and than is man xxxvi. He may assende no more for than hathe nature gyuen hym beauty and strength at the full / and repyd the sedes of perfet vnderstondynge.
>
> Than cometh Iulii that oure fruytes ben sette a sonnynge & oure corne a-hardenynge. But than the sone begyneth a lytell for to descende downewarde so man than goeth fro youthe towoward age and begynneth for to aquaynt hym with sadnes / for than he is two and forty yere.[16]

No wonder Spenser called his poem *The Shepheardes Calender*, with all its woodcuts and wonderful matters, poetical, philosophical, and theological.

So too with Robert Herrick's *Hesperides*, in its own way a compost or Kalender, even though it computes only what Herrick calls "The succession of the foure sweet months," thus:

> First, *April*, she with mellow showrs
> Opens the way for early flowers;
> Then after her comes smiling *May*,
> In a more rich and sweet aray:

Next enters *June*, and brings us more
Jems, then those two, that went before:
Then (lastly) *July* comes, and she
More wealth brings in, then all those three.[17]

That is the complete poem: a pastoral purification of the seasons—
though Herrick, as many of his other poems show, knows well the
seasons of cold, decay, and death. Despite the incredible variety
displayed in the 1,130 poems (mostly very short) in his book,[18]
Hesperides comes, "piece by piece," under the control of the pastoral ideal that Herrick sets forth at the forefront of his book as
he addresses his muse. "Whither *Mad maiden* wilt thou roame?"
he asks (p. 12), and roam she surely does, toward imagined, but
never achieved, dalliance with his "many fresh and fragrant Mis-
tresses" (p. 284)—a gallery of all those girls for whom the ancient
poets pined:

Stately *Julia*, prime of all;
Sapho next, a principall:
Smooth *Anthea*, for a skin
White, and Heaven-like Chrystalline:
Sweet *Electra*, and the choice
Myrha, for the Lute, and Voice.
Next, *Corinna*, for her wit,
And the graceful use of it:
With *Perilla*: All are gone;
Onely *Herrick's* left alone,
For to number sorrow by
Their departures hence, and die.

[p. 25]

He often also turns to their contraries, those loathsome crea-
tures with bad breath that haunt his scurrilous epigrams: "First,
Jollies wife is lame; then next, loose-hipt: / Squint-ey'd, hook-
nos'd; and lastly, Kidney-lipt." (p. 91) His muse roams to ponder
the ravages of civil war and constantly ponders death in all its
guises, but at the heart lies the pastoral *modus* of the master shepherd:

Whither *Mad maiden* wilt thou roame?
Farre safer 'twere to stay at home . . .
There with the Reed, thou mayst expresse
The Shepherds Fleecie happinesse:
And with thy *Eclogues* intermixe
Some smooth, and harmlesse *Beucolicks*.
There on a Hillock thou mayst sing
Unto a handsome Shephardling;
Or to a Girle (that keeps the Neat)
With breath more sweet then Violet.
There, there, (perhaps) such Lines as These
May take the simple *Villages*.
But for the Court, the Country wit
Is despicable unto it.
Stay then at home, and doe not goe
Or flie abroad to seeke for woe. . . .
That man's unwise will search for Ill,
And may prevent it, sitting still.

[p. 12]

Sitting still, in the pastoral shade, Herrick's muse can denounce the dullness and crudeness of Devonshire in certain pieces, but then the major poems of the volume return to, and maintain, the pastoral center: "*Corinna's* Going a Maying," poems on the joy and peace and contentment of the country life, wedding songs, festival poems for the harvest home and other rural celebrations, along with poems formally entitled "Pastorall," "Eclogue," or "Bucolick." Through poems like these the pastoral vision tempers and purifies, until at the close Herrick can write: "To his Book's end this last line he'd have plac't, / *Jocond his Muse was; but his Life was chast.*" To prove the point a slender bunch of his "Pious Pieces" is tacked on after his "Book's end," "Noble Numbers" from the Christian world that have been expurgated from the pastoral garden, pious weeds that would impair the pagan flowers.

So too in Shakespeare's *Winter's Tale* we find the pastoral episode of Perdita set in between two courtly scenes, between the tragic, blasphemous jealousy of Leontes and the later scene of

resurrection and reconciliation, but it is, we must note, the purified vision of the pastoral episode that makes possible the healing
and reconciliation. In Bohemia, that never-never land, the rogue
Autolycus merrily cheats and steals as he presides over the sheep-
shearing festival with happy songs that bring joy and harmony to
the rustics; he sings of lying with his "aunts" in the hay, but
we never witness any such activities. All the threats of the outer
world are mentioned, and indeed they are menacingly present in
the figure of the disguised king who, at the close, will shatter
the pastoral harmony. While the pastoral vision prevails, all of
these potential harms come under the spell. The king himself ad-
mires the pastoral maiden and gently converses with her about
nature and art, while she, the symbol of pure pastoral, refuses to
grow gilliflowers from slips. When both Florizel and Perdita sing
those old Ovidian myths—which have, at this stage of literary
history, thoroughly merged with all pastoral actions—the legends
lose their uglier aspects and become purified:

> The gods themselves,
> Humbling their deities to love, have taken
> The shapes of beasts upon them: Jupiter
> Became a bull, and bellow'd; the green Neptune
> A ram, and bleated; and the fire-rob'd god,
> Golden Apollo, a poor humble swain,
> As I seem now.
>
> [IV.iv.25–31][19]

They have blended into the pastoral scene, their lusts subdued:

> Their transformations
> Were never for a piece of beauty rarer,
> Nor in a way so chaste, since my desires
> Run not before mine honour, nor my lusts
> Burn hotter than my faith.
>
> [IV.iv.31–35]

And the gods in Perdita's great flower speech likewise submit to
the pastoral control:

> O Proserpina,
> For the flowers now that, frighted, thou let'st fall
> From Dis's waggon! daffodils,
> That come before the swallow dares, and take
> The winds of March with beauty; violets, dim,
> But sweeter than the lids of Juno's eyes
> Or Cytherea's breath . . .

[IV.iv.116–22]

While her vision is set on springtime flowers, the violence of Pluto and the sad long search of Ceres for her daughter fall away into the background; the violent, destructive jealousy that so often rages in the eyes of Ovid's Juno is hidden beneath her sweet eyelids, and the raging power of *amor* in the reign of Ovid's Venus fades away into Cytherea's fragrant breath. Robert Herrick, we might note in passing, performs much the same purification in his poem "The Apron of Flowers," in which Sappha, like Proserpina, gathers into her apron the flowers of the spring:

> Her Apron gave (as she did passe)
> An Odor more divine,
> More pleasing too, then ever was
> The lap of *Proserpine.*

The pastoral vision knows of the violence that lurks within the flowery field of Enna, but while the vision lasts, it renders these evils ineffectual.

This is clear in the last great pastoral action to be written under the impulse of the European Renaissance: John Milton's vision of Paradise in the fourth book of *Paradise Lost.* Here too is the pastoral center that purifies. With inward eyes illumined in answer to his prayer, the bard of the poem sees the earthly paradise, with Satan already there, adopting various metamorphic disguises, although Satan is not yet successful in his destructive intent. Adam and Eve are there, the original of all pastoral lovers, and the whole range of pastoral and Ovidian literature is ransacked for allusion and brought here into one last Kalender of "grateful vicissitude" without mortality. Ovid's myths, like Satan, lurk everywhere, but while the vision holds, they are deprived of any "noxious" power. Thus Eve, like Narcissus, sees her image in a beautiful pool beneath a pastoral shade, but, unlike Narcissus, who ignores the warning of the poet's voice, Eve heeds the voices of God and Adam and then goes on to declare her love for Adam in the first of all pastoral love songs. It is a poem in which, like the shepherds of Vergil and Theocritus, she seems to engage in a singing contest, though the competition lies within herself, as she weaves her skillful, alternate song:

> Sweet is the breath of morn, her rising sweet,
> With charm of earliest Birds; pleasant the Sun
> When first on this delightful Land he spreads
> His orient Beams, on herb, tree, fruit, and flour,
> Glistring with dew; fragrant the fertil earth
> After soft showers; and sweet the coming on
> Of grateful Eevning milde, then silent Night
> With this her solemn Bird and this fair Moon,
> And these the Gemms of Heav'n, her starrie train:
> But neither breath of Morn when she ascends
> With charm of earliest Birds, nor rising Sun
> On this delightful land, nor herb, fruit, floure,
> Glistring with dew, nor fragrance after showers,
> Nor grateful Evening mild, nor silent Night
> With this her solemn Bird, nor walk by Moon,
> Or glittering Starr-light without thee is sweet.
>
> [IV, 641–56][20]

Though the two parts of this alternate song are not equal in length, I believe we can hear behind its repetitions a distant echo of the singing match in Vergil's seventh eclogue, with its catalogue of trees and the ancient pastoral topos in which nature's beauty depends upon the beloved's presence:

Corydon. Hercules loves poplars best of all; Bacchus prefers the vine; Venus, the Queen of Beauty, loves the myrtle best; and Apollo his own bays. Phyllis is fond of hazels. As long as Phyllis likes them best, neither the myrtle nor Apollo's bays shall take a higher place than hazels.

Thyrsis. The ash in forests is the loveliest tree; the pine in gardens; the poplar by the river's bank; and the fir-tree on the mountain-heights. But if you, my handsome Lycidas, will spend more time with me, the ash in her own forest and the pine-tree in the garden must give place to you.[21]

So pastoral art lives in Milton's paradise—a vision that stands as the healing center for mankind's heavy loss.

Such, then, is the constant function of pastoral: to preserve a center of values. I was reminded of this once again by a performance of *Don Giovanni* in the Opera Festival at Durham while I was composing this essay. Zerlina is the healing center; as she kneels by her rustic lover, who has been badly beaten by the seducer, she hears Masetto count all his wounds from head to toe and then she sings: "Well then there's still a lot of you that's healthy." This is the constant message of pastoral to a troubled world.

NOTES

1. Robert Penn Warren, *Selected Essays* (New York: Random House, 1958), pp. 3–31, esp. pp. 4, 26–27.

2. Text from Milton's *Mask* in his *Poems*, 1645.

3. Ovid, *Metamorphoses*, 3.341–510; 6.519–48.

4. Ibid., 14.320–96.

5. *Englands Helicon*, edited by Hyder Edward Rollins, 2 vols. (Cambridge: Harvard University Press, 1935), 1:27–28.

6. Quoted from Rollins's notes to his edition of *Englands Helicon*, 2:89.

7. *The Poems of Theocritus*, translated by Anna Rist (Chapel Hill: University of North Carolina Press, 1978). I am indebted to the translator's commentary on this idyll and also to the study by Gilbert Lawall, *Theocritus' Coan Pastorals* (Cambridge: Harvard University Press, 1967), pp. 16–33.

8. Vergil, Eclogue I, 51–58; in the translation by E. V. Rieu, *Virgil: The Pastoral Poems* (Harmondsworth: Penguin Books, 1954). Subsequent translations from the *Eclogues* are, with a few exceptions, by Rieu; Latin quotations are taken from Vergil's *Opera*, edited by F. A. Hirtzel (Oxford: Clarendon Press, 1900).

9. William Berg, *Early Virgil* (London: Athlone Press, 1974), pp. 155–77, esp. pp. 166–67: "The poem does not maintain a solemn tone throughout, and often exhibits the character of a bucolic *ludus* . . ." Berg goes on to argue that the *puer* is "Virgil's literary hero of the future" (p. 170).

10. I follow here the reading of the Hirtzel text; for a convincing defence of this reading against the variant *cui . . . parentes*, see the edition of the *Eclogues* by Robert Coleman (Cambridge: Cambridge University Press, 1977), pp. 148–49.

11. See Charles Paul Segal, *Landscape in Ovid's Metamorphoses, Hermes: Einzelschriften*, 23 (Wiesbaden, 1969), esp. section IV.

12. See Michael C. J. Putnam, *Virgil's Pastoral Art* (Princeton: Princeton University Press, 1970), pp. 293–341.

13. See *The Kalender of Shepherdes*, edited by H. Oskar Sommer, 3 vols. (London: Kegan Paul, 1892), 1:32, where Sommer reprints the prologue of the translator, Robert Copland, for Wynkyn de Worde's edition of 1508. Sommer's edition includes a facsimile of the English version of 1503 and a reprint of Pynson's edition of 1506. The following quotations are taken from Pynson's version, in Sommer's reprint, with slight changes in punctuation and capitalization. For the history of the work, see Sommer, *Kalender*, vol. 1, and Helen Cooper, *Pastoral: Mediaeval into Renaissance* (Ipswich: D. S. Brewer, 1977), pp. 71–72, 78–79, 186.

14. Sommer, *Kalender*, 3:12.

15. Ibid., 1:101.

16. Ibid., 3:11.

17. *The Complete Poetry of Robert Herrick*, edited by J. Max Patrick (New York: W. W. Norton, 1968), p. 35. Page numbers following quotations from Herrick refer to this edition.

18. I refer here to the "pagan" part of Herrick's volume, *Hesperides* properly so called, though the general title page uses *Hesperides* to cover his "Works Both Humane and Divine"—that is, both *Hesperides* and the appended *Noble Numbers*. For the phrase "piece by piece," see "The Argument of his Book," line 7.

19. Text from the Arden edition of *The Winter's Tale*, edited by J. H. P. Pafford (London: Methuen, 1963).

20. Text from *The Student's Milton*, edited by Frank Allen Patterson (New York: Crofts, 1930).

21. *Eclogues*, 7.61–68. I owe this suggestion to my colleague Gordon Williams. For a more detailed discussion of Eve's love song in relation to Ovid and the pastoral tradition, see my *Poet of Exile: A Study of Milton's Poetry* (New Haven: Yale University Press, 1980), pp. 220–26.

V

Abraham and the Reformation: The Controversy over Pauline Interpretation in the Early Sixteenth Century

David C. Steinmetz
Duke University

The story of the Old Testament patriarch, Abraham, plays a central role in two of the major religious disputes of the sixteenth century.[1] One dispute, curiously enough, concerns the relation of Abraham to the rite of circumcision and is mainly confined to certain Protestants of a generally Calvinist orientation who support infant baptism and to other more radical Protestants, primarily Anabaptists, who vigorously oppose it.[2] Abraham becomes for the German and Swiss Reformed a symbol of the continuity of the people of God in history and of the gradual transition rather than abrupt disjuncture which separates the Old Testament from the New. It is a fascinating debate and one whose importance for the history of Protestantism in the sixteenth century cannot be sufficiently stressed. Nevertheless, it is a dispute which we shall for the moment ignore.

The second debate, and the one with which we shall concern ourselves, actually antedates the Protestant Reformation and is stimulated by a quotation from the Pentateuch (Genesis 15:6): "Abraham believed God and it was reckoned to him for righteousness." St. Paul was fascinated with this quotation and used it to undercut the arguments of Jewish Christians who wished to bar from membership in the church all Gentiles who had not first embraced a kind of minimal Judaism.[3] Against these Jewish Christians, Paul argued that Abraham was accounted righteous by God, not because he had submitted to the rite of circumcision and not because he kept the moral and ceremonial precepts of the Torah (Abraham, after all, was dust long before Moses was born), but because he trusted a promise given to him by God.

What made Abraham's faith so remarkable in Paul's estimation was that the promise defied ordinary human expectation. Abraham was promised a son whose offspring would become, in the language of the anonymous author of Genesis, as numberless as the sands of the seashore or the stars in the heavens. Abraham was an old man when he received this promise and a much older man before he saw its realization. To compound his difficulties still further, Abraham was married to an aging and chronically infertile woman. When Sarah, his wife, first heard of the promise to Abraham, she laughed. That seems, on the face of it, not a totally inappropriate response.

But Abraham, to use the happy phrase of Erasmus, united two contraries; that is to say, he "hoped in things despaired of."[4] He had utter confidence in a God who creates fresh possibilities for the faithful where all ordinary human possibilities have been exhausted. This unconditional trust in the promise of God, a trust which flew in the teeth of the accumulated contrary evidence, became the basis on which God acknowledged Abraham as a righteous man.

The conclusion which Paul drew from this story was enormously significant for the self-understanding of the early church. If Abraham had been justified by faith rather than by the rite of circumcision or the observance of the Torah, then a relationship to God based on faith is more fundamental than a relationship based on adherence to a code of moral and ceremonial precepts. There is a sense, then, in which Christianity with its stress on faith in God's promises antedates Judaism with its emphasis on obedience to the Law. Gentiles who stand in a relationship of faith to God are in a certain sense children of Abraham and are permitted immediate access to baptism and membership in the covenant people of God. They are not obliged to undergo a prior and preparatory conversion to Judaism. That is not all that St. Paul has to say about Abraham but it is enough to give you the flavor of his argument.

[95]

With the decline of Jewish Christianity and with a corresponding decline in a largely Gentile church of interest in the relationship between Christianity and post-biblical Judaism, the argument
of Paul was put to other uses. The problem for Christian theology
after the death of Paul was no longer the relationship between
Israel and the church but rather what constituted the proper relationship between faith and works. After all, while Paul insisted
that Abraham was justified by his faith, James argued just as dog-
gedly that Abraham was justified by works. How were these apparently contradictory assertions to be reconciled?

The thesis that Abraham was justified by his faith became in-
creasingly problematic in a church which distinguished between
fides informis and *fides formata*, *fides implicita* and *fides explicita*, *fides
quae* and *fides qua*, *fides acquisita* and *fides infusa*, *credulitas* and *fidu-
cia*. When Genesis 15:6 spoke of the faith of Abraham, did it have
in mind *credere Deum*, *credere Deo*, or *credere in Deum*? What was
the relationship between Abraham's faith, however understood,
and the Old Testament sacrament of circumcision? Did circumcision have a causative role *ex opere operantis* or *ex opere operato*, *ex natura rei* or *ex pacto Dei*? Or was circumcision merely a sign and not,
properly speaking, a sacrament at all? Questions such as these,
which would have perplexed St. Paul, came gradually to replace
the older issues generated by the separation of Christianity from
its Jewish environment.

In spite of the importance of Pauline interpretation for the history of the church, relatively little attention has been paid to it by
historians.[5] This neglect poses an especially acute problem for students of the Reformation since theologians in the sixteenth century devoted themselves to a study of the letters of Paul with an
intensity unprecedented in the history of the Christian church.[6]
Protestants are frequently credited with this revival of interest in
Pauline literature, and it is true that Protestants contributed a dis-
proportionate share of the commentaries on Paul; but the renaissance in Pauline studies was well under way before the Reformation began as the writings of Ficino, Erasmus, Colet, and Lefèvre
d'Étaples amply testify. While Catholic commentators on Paul are
not so numerous as Protestant exegetes, significant commentaries

on Paul were written by such important and influential cardinals as Cajetan,[7] Sadoleto,[8] and Seripando.[9]

It would not be possible in a single paper to sketch the whole sweep of Pauline studies in the early sixteenth century or even to summarize the weight of sixteenth-century scholarly opinion on each of the many themes developed by Paul in the course of his epistles, but it would be possible and, I hope, profitable to take one theme—namely, the crucial problem of Abraham's justification by faith—and to show three important moments in the history of the interpretation of that single theme.

I have chosen three commentators, two Germans and an Italian, who did not know each other personally but who had common ties nonetheless and who embodied theological tendencies in the interpretation of Paul consciously opposed by the other two. The first commentator is Wendelin Steinbach (1454–1519),[10] professor of theology at the University of Tübingen, who lectured on Paul's letter to the Galatians in 1513.[11] Steinbach was the foremost disciple of the German nominalist theologian, Gabriel Biel, and the editor of his published works. Indeed, Steinbach so subordinated his career to the career of his master that his own lectures on the Bible were never published during his lifetime. Steinbach represents an approach to Paul which reflects the theological presuppositions of German nominalism.

The second commentator, not surprisingly, is Martin Luther (1483–1546), professor of biblical studies at the University of Wittenberg. Luther was thoroughly trained at Erfurt in the theology of Gabriel Biel and reacted violently against it. He lectured on Romans in 1515–16, Galatians in 1516 and 1531, and on the Abraham stories in Genesis in 1538–39. In his lectures on Paul, Luther rejected point by point the main assertions about Abraham advanced by Steinbach. Even though Luther did not read Steinbach's lectures, he correctly anticipated the exegetical points which Steinbach had made. While later Protestant commentators did not slavishly repeat Luther's exegesis of Romans 4 and Galatians 3, they did accept—as the commentaries of Zwingli,[12] Bullinger,[13] Brenz,[14] Melanchthon,[15] and Calvin[16] demonstrate—the thrust of Luther's argument.

The last commentator is Girolamo Cardinal Seripando (1493–1563), general of the Augustinian Order, archbishop of Salerno, and papal legate to the Council of Trent.[17] Seripando had been commissioned by Pope Paul III to make a special study of the writings of the Protestants so that the theological points raised by them could be intelligently addressed. He was sympathetic to the Augustinianism of the Protestants, though it was in his opinion an Augustinianism which had lost its Catholic bearings and had therefore seriously misinterpreted the original sources to which it appealed. He was one of the most influential figures at the Council of Trent and, even though some of his opinions on original sin and justification were not finally accepted, he nevertheless shaped the outcome of the important conciliar decisions on those topics. In his posthumously published commentaries on Romans and Galatians, Seripando rejected the exegesis of such Catholic interpreters as Steinbach and such Protestant interpreters as Luther. He tried to find a Catholic middle way between a reading of Paul which conceded too much to Pelagius and one which broke too sharply with antecedent tradition.

The clash of these three competing interpretations of Paul, particularly of Paul's teaching concerning the faith of Abraham, is a fundamental dispute and is regarded by the commentators themselves as ultimately irreconcilable. The dispute is intense because each interpretation of Paul presupposes, contains, and implies a competing vision of the nature of the religious life. In this argument the figure of Abraham, who was a symbol for Paul of what united Jews and Gentiles in a common faith, becomes for sixteenth-century interpreters of Paul a symbol of what separates Protestant from Catholic, heretic from orthodox, the truly devout from the ungodly.

During the last years of his life, Wendelin Steinbach, who represented Occamist theology at Tübingen from 1486 to 1517, found his theological assumptions challenged to the hilt by his study of the epistles of Paul and by his wide reading in the Amerbach edition of the writings of Augustine.[18] Steinbach had been taught by his mentor, Gabriel Biel, that sinners could, by the proper use of

their natural moral endowments, earn the first grace of justification by a merit of congruity.[19] Such a view came perilously close to
the Pelagian views which Augustine had so roundly condemned.
Not that Biel thought for one moment that his views were Pelagian! On the contrary, he was convinced that he had added all the
proper Augustinian safeguards to his doctrine of grace to preserve
it from any such charge.

Still the concentrated reading of massive doses of Augustine
and Paul proved unsettling for Biel's erstwhile disciple, Steinbach,
who was more accustomed to deal with their writings as a series
of vetted quotations in a manual of theology. But Paul and Augustine, taken in context and at face value, held positions which
directly conflicted with the fundamental principles of Occamist
thought. It was all very unnerving for Steinbach, who would have
preferred to discover that all his favorite authors sweetly harmonized with each other. Instead, Steinbach found that his most important ancient authorities clashed dreadfully with his most es-
teemed modern ones.

The problem, however, was largely a hermeneutical one.[20]
Steinbach was willing to concede (who, after all, could deny it)
that certain opinions of Paul and Augustine, if taken at face value,
could not be harmonized with certain opinions of Biel, but then,
too, not everything uttered by Paul pleased Augustine in its stark
and unqualified form. Even the old Augustine found it necessary
to go through his earlier writings with a blue pencil, adding foot-
notes and marginal notations. In short, theological language is
historically conditioned. It is affected by the pastoral or polemical
situation in which the theologian finds himself when he writes.[21]
Ways of talking about God which are appropriate and useful in
one historical epoch may prove misleading, even dangerous, in
another.[22]

It is possible to take any number of examples of the historical character of theological language from the writings of Augustine.[23] For example, Augustine appears to deny that human moral
activity can be virtuous or good *de genere* without the gift of infused love.[24] While Steinbach admits that infused charity belongs
to the substance of the act of loving God and that good works

should have a habitual relationship to God as their final end, he is not willing to deny free will or virtue to sinners who are still outside a state of grace.[25] If the literal sense of Augustine's proposition is true—no virtue without charity—then it is impossible for a sinner to earn justifying grace by a merit of congruity, a position Steinbach wants desperately to maintain. If one distinguishes, however, between Augustine's way of speaking and the real content of his theology, this tension is dissipated and Augustine can be shown to harmonize with the best Occamist theology.[26]

What is true of Augustine is also true of Paul.[27] When Paul asserts that Abraham was justified by his faith and implies that Abraham was justified by faith alone, he is putting forward a claim which any competent theologian knows is not true. James 2[28] as well as I Corinthians 3 and 13[29] demonstrates that the faith which justifies is a faith formed by love (*fides caritate formata*).[30] Steinbach is enough of an Occamist to believe that there is no inherent power in charity which by its own nature merits eternal beatitude. The law that a sinner must have a habit of grace is a regulation established freely by the ordained power of God. Love, therefore, has no necessary causality but only a causality *sine qua non*.[31] Still it is infused love and not faith which is the real principle of justification.[32] What on earth could Paul have meant when he claimed that Abraham was reckoned as righteous by God on no other ground than his faith?

What we have here, in Steinbach's opinion, is a particularly outrageous example of Paul's peculiar *modus loquendi*. When Paul says that Abraham is justified by faith and implies by this that Abraham is justified by faith alone, he is using a way of talking appropriate for catechumens who are not yet fully aware that faith alone (in the sense of unformed or acquired faith) cannot save.[33] Only faith working by love saves. St. Paul knew that as well as St. James. What St. Paul is claiming (and we must be careful not to miss his point or be thrown off by his incautious phraseology) is that Abraham merited the first grace of justification by his good works, preeminently by the good work of believing God with his unformed faith.[34]

In other words, the career of Abraham is an illustration of the theological principle which Biel cites with great regularity: "God does not deny his grace to those who do what is in them." Abraham did what was in him.[35] He was a virtuous man who struggled to love the God who had called him from Ur of the Chaldees and who grasped the promises of God with his own unformed and therefore imperfect faith. He performed works which were good *de genere* and by them merited the infused love which would form his faith and make it saving.[36]

If Paul meant only to suggest that Abraham merited grace by his unformed faith, why did he express himself in such a careless and exaggerated way in Romans 4 and Galatians 3? The answer for Steinbach lies in the mystery of divine providence. The excessive language of Paul (not excessive, of course, if one knows how to read it properly) concerning the faith of Abraham provided the later Pelagian heretics no foundation in Paul's letters to which they could rightfully appeal in support of their ideas.[37] The theological situation of the church in the first four centuries dictated the kind of polemical rhetoric at which Paul was master.

Now, however, that the Pelagian heresy has been met and successfully weathered by the church, the need for more restrained and precise theological language requires the church to rephrase the moderate intentions of Paul in forms appropriate to their real meaning. Theologians *post Pelagium* can, without eroding the authority of either Paul or Augustine, use language and formulations which they themselves *ante Pelagium* would have rejected.[38]

When the text from Genesis which Paul quotes says that "Abraham believed God and it was reckoned to him for righteousness," it means that Abraham believed God with an unformed faith which earned the gift of infused love. He earned it, of course, *de congruo* and not *de condigno*, but merit it he did. Once having merited the gift of love, Abraham could believe God with a formed faith and be in the full sense of the term a righteous man. Indeed, one can find no better illustration of the nominalist view that sinners merit grace by their virtue than the Pauline image of Abraham.

[101]

There is scarcely a point which Steinbach makes which Luther does not take some pains to deny. He rejects, for example, the contention that Paul and Augustine defended exaggerated theological positions out of pastoral or polemical necessity.[39] Luther sees no need for a new hermeneutic to adjust the historically conditioned teaching of the ancient church fathers to modern circumstances,[40] certainly no need for a hermeneutic which can with a clear conscience interpret Abraham as the model pilgrim of nominalist soteriology. The teaching of Paul is true as it stands. The hermeneutical problem is not how to adjust or modify the teaching of Paul so that it will become intelligible to people who customarily think in modern philosophical and theological categories but rather how to modify the modern reader's customary ways of thinking and talking about God so that he can begin to grasp the astonishing and wholly unexpected message of Paul. In Luther's view it is scholastic theology and not the New Testament which needs to be subjected to radical hermeneutical surgery.[41]

When asked to discuss what the New Testament means by faith, Luther seizes on the language of Hebrews 11:1 as the most appropriate vocabulary for explaining its nature: "Faith is the substance of things hoped for, the evidence of things unseen." If one examines this biblical definition of faith through the lenses provided by Aristotelian philosophy, one will seriously misunderstand what is being said.[42] When the Bible talks about substance, it is not talking about the essence or quiddity of a thing.[43] It is talking about what stands under a person, about a supporting foundation upon which one can build one's life.[44] Sinners have the substance of their lives in visible objects which they can see, touch, catalogue, buy, exploit, cherish, destroy, or sell.[45] The godly have their substance in things that cannot be seen, things that can only be believed or hoped for.[46] Believers build their lives on promises unsupported by empirical evidence and very probably contradicted by it.[47] Therefore faith seems an incredibly stupid enterprise to sane and sensible people who are not (as they understand themselves) swayed by emotion or sentiment and who cling with both hands to solid and incontrovertible facts.[48]

When Luther insists that the object of faith is invisible, he does so for two reasons, neither of which has very much to do with Plato or with heavenly archetypes. The object of faith is invisible either because it is future (who of us can see next Wednesday) or because it is hidden in the present under the form of a contrary and contradictory appearance.[49] Luther is quite certain in his own mind that the New Testament speaks of a God who is deliberately and simultaneously hidden and revealed, hidden in fact in his very revelation. This simultaneity of hiddenness and revelation makes faith a much more complex phenomenon than Steinbach ever dreamed it could be.

In other words, it is not apparent to sight that the promise to Abraham of a son is anything more than a wistful projection by a childless old man; or that Abraham's search for a new homeland is anything nobler than a quest for better pasture for his cattle and sheep; or that his abortive attempt to offer his son, Isaac, as a human sacrifice is anything other than an act of primitive and misguided religious fanaticism. Yet the Bible, against reason and common sense, claims that Abraham was justified precisely because he was not sane and sensible. He believed a promise to which no prudent and responsible man would have given credence and, by doing so, became such an object of divine mercy and love that the angels (if they could indulge in envy) might have been jealous of him. The presence of God was discerned by Abraham, not by sight, but by hearing the word of promise which contradicted the evidence his eyes could see all too clearly and by trusting it.[50] Abraham's faith justified him because it was formed by the word of God which he unreservedly and unconditionally trusted. In his scholion on Hebrews 11:8, Luther observes:

But this is the glory of faith, simply not to know: not to know where you are going, not to know what you are doing, not to know what you must suffer, and with sense and intellect, virtue and will, all alike made captive, to follow the naked voice of God, to be led and driven, rather than to go. And thus it is clear, that Abraham with this obedience of faith shows the highest example of the evangelical life, because he left all and followed the Lord, preferring the Word of God to everything else and loving it above all things; of his own free will a pilgrim, and subject to the perils of life and death every hour of the day and night.[51]

Central to Luther's early thought is the correlation of Word and faith. The God of the Old and New Testaments is a God who enters into covenants and who makes promises.[52] When Scripture speaks of the truth of God, it has in mind the unbroken and un-breakable fidelity of God to his promises.[53] These promises are grasped by faith. Since, however, the promises are to a very large extent testimonies concerning matters still pending in the future, faith has more the character of hope than the character of mem-ory. Those people who are justified by faith have, as Luther says, all their goods in words and promises.[54] Their substance,[55] the ground on which they build their lives, is the invisible reality of the "things which do not appear"—invisible either because they are future or because they are hidden in the present under the jarring and discordant form of contrary appearance.

Since the promises of God touch matters which contradict rea-son, sight, common sense, Luther is willing to talk rather para-doxically about justifying God as a way of justifying the self. Since God is just already, he does not need to be justified by sinners. Nevertheless, God *is* justified in his words when people trust his promise of grace for the humble.[56] By conforming their judgments to the judgment of God against the contrary evidence of reason and common sense,[57] they confess that God is true and risk their lives on his promises.[58] By justifying God in this way, they are themselves in turn justified by God.

The proper disposition for such justification is prayer. The sin-ner cries out for salvation,[59] groans like Christian before he has opened the wicket gate, and awaits with eager expectancy on God, who is truthful and cannot lie, to make good on his prom-ises. The verbs that give theological content to the old axiom about "doing what is in one" are "ask," "seek," "knock."[60] Lu-ther's sinners accuse themselves of sin and justify God in his judg-ment. It is by becoming a "real sinner" that Luther takes advan-tage of the good news that the only thing the sinner has to offer in exchange for grace—namely, his ingrown and besetting sin—is ex-actly what God asks him to give.[61] The gospel is not "give me your virtue and I will crown it with grace" but "despise your sin and I will shower you with mercy." To suggest that Abraham merited the first grace of justification by his virtuous activity and his unformed faith is to turn the gospel on its head.

Luther, who believes that justification is by naked trust in the fragile, apparently contradictory, and largely unsubstantiated promises of God, regards Abraham as an example of an "absolute believer." By "absolute believer" Luther has reference more to the scope of Abraham's faith than to its constancy. Abraham is justified, not because he believes this or that promise of God, but because he stands ready to believe *any* promise of God, no matter how violently it may contradict the judgments of his own prudential reason and common sense.[62] Abraham's faith is not so much an act (e.g., believing that Sarah will become pregnant in spite of her advanced years) as a disposition (e.g., believing that whatever God promises, however startling, he is able to perform). Steinbach's translation of Abraham's faith into a pious work is, on Luther's principles, a fundamental misreading of Paul.

Luther sums up his views concerning the faith of Abraham in his 1538 lectures on Genesis:

> Then what? Is the Law useless for righteousness? Yes, certainly. But does faith alone, without works, justify? Yes, certainly. Otherwise you must repudiate Moses, who declares that Abraham is righteous prior to the Law and prior to the works of the Law, not because he sacrificed his son, who had not yet been born, and not because he did this or that work, but because he believed God who gave a promise.
>
> In this passage no mention is made of any preparation for grace, of any faith formed through works, or of any preceding disposition. This, however, is mentioned: that at that time Abraham was in the midst of sins, doubts, and fears, and was exceedingly troubled in spirit.
>
> How, then, did he obtain righteousness? In this way: God speaks and Abraham believes what God is saying.[63]

Our last commentator will detain us only briefly. Not that Girolamo Cardinal Seripando was not important and did not write a significant commentary on Romans and Galatians, but rather as C. S. Lewis once observed, things need to be explained at length not in proportion to their importance but in proportion to their difficulty.

Seripando accepted neither Steinbach's image of Abraham as

an Occamist pilgrim who earned the first grace of justification by his unformed faith and his virtuous acts nor Luther's portrait of Abraham as the "absolute believer" who risked his life on a promise of God and so was justified by faith alone. In Seripando's opinion, Paul makes it quite clear that works which precede justifying faith are works "according to the flesh" (*secundum carnem*).[64] Fleshly works do not justify nor, as Steinbach suggested, is righteousness ever imputed to them by a merit of congruity.[65] Seripando is very sympathetic to Luther's ferocious attack on the Pelagianizing tendencies of German nominalism and agrees in the main with Luther's Augustinian protest.

But Luther's constructive alternative to Steinbach is itself seriously flawed. Abraham was not justified by faith alone[66] because St. James is adamant that faith without works is dead.[67] The faith which justified Abraham was a faith which worked by love.[68] However, such faith is not a natural endowment.[69] It is a gift of God which is bestowed without antecedent human merit. The faith with which Abraham pleased God was not something that Abraham offered to God as a pious work but a gift which God both conceded and accepted.[70]

Faith is therefore the entrance to righteousness,[71] but the believer is not justified by faith alone since faith is perfected by love and by the virtues which flow from love. Abraham is justified by faith (which is a gift and not a natural human faculty) and this faith is in turn consummated in works of charity.[72] Faith must be, to use the Latin terms which Seripando employs, *actuosa non ociosa, operosa non languida, viva non mortua*.[73] Faith is related to works as a beginning to the end, as a foundation to the building erected upon it, as the root of a plant to the fruit which it finally bears.[74]

When Paul uses such words as "impute" and "non-imputation," he does not have in mind the forensic doctrine of justification taught by Luther, Bucer, Calvin, and the rest of the magisterial Protestants. What he means rather is this: "To impute is to ascribe to a man what he neither has nor can have by the power of human nature, such as faith for righteousness: since faith is beyond any man and since no one can fully merit righteousness, which does not operate according to a scheme of reward. Not to impute, however, is not to attribute to a man what he both has by a fault of nature and cannot get rid of by the powers of nature, such as sin. Concerning this, David said, 'Blessed is the man to whom the Lord does not impute sin.' "[75] In short, what Seripando is eager to revive against both the Pelagianizing tendencies of Steinbach and the far too innovative and untraditional theology of Luther is the ancient and venerable Augustinian tradition of the interpretation of Paul, a tradition which emphasizes *sola gratia* against Steinbach and *fides caritate formata* against Luther.

There you have it, three distinct and competing views of the meaning of Abraham's faith. Depending whether you believe Steinbach or Luther or Seripando, Paul teaches that Abraham did or did not earn grace by his good works, was or was not justified by faith alone, did or did not find the perfection of his faith in works of charity. One should learn from the example of Abraham—again depending upon which reading of Paul one finds convincing—to "do what is in one" in order to merit the first grace of infused love or to abandon all confidence in one's own good works and cling to the promises of God by faith alone or to make sure that the faith which one professes is a faith which works by love. Three models of piety are implied by the three images of Abraham and it is necessary for the faithful to make a discriminating choice between them. It is not possible to embrace all three at once.

That much is obvious, but there are some other aspects of this controversy which do not lie so clearly on the surface, and I should like to conclude by making a few brief observations about them.

1. There are certain Protestant interpreters of the New Testament who are inclined to believe that the meaning of any biblical text is virtually, if not altogether, identical with the original intention of the author of that text. Since Steinbach, Luther, and Seripando have not placed their interpretations of Romans 4 and Galatians 3 in the original context created by the separation of early Christianity from its Jewish matrix, they have simply misunderstood Paul and their exegesis should be quietly buried in the

nearest available wastepaper basket. The meaning of a text is exhausted by the intention of the original author of that text.

That is, of course, to place a demand on the Bible which no sensible person would think of placing on any other literary text. Even granting what I am not readily prepared to grant, that it is an easy matter to recapture the original intention of an ancient author, a good literary text creates a field of meanings and associations not explicitly worked out in the mind of the author but implicitly contained in the text itself. In the interaction of reader and text, those implicit meanings are discerned and brought to expression. The meaning of a text is defined in part by the intention of the author as it is in part by the prior meanings of the words which he uses, but new experiences cast new light on old texts.

2. I do not wish to suggest that a text has no proper meaning of its own but can mean anything that an interpreter, provided his imagination is virile enough to overcome the inhibitions of his conscience, wants it to mean. There was, for example, some brave talk in the later Middle Ages by theologians who had been seriously frightened by Wycliffite and Hussite readings of the Bible that the church could, under the inspiration of the Holy Spirit, choose the less grammatical meaning of a biblical text as its true theological significance. That is a hypothesis easier to embrace as an abstract principle than it is to employ in a concrete instance.

In point of fact, the church or, perhaps I should say, Christian churches of whatever kind have found it exceedingly difficult to contend for very long against the plain historical-grammatical meaning of the words of Scripture. While no interpreter is bound to the original intention of the author as the sole meaning of a biblical text, one is bound by that intention to a limited field of possible meanings. Steinbach's interpretation of Paul was the interpretation most difficult to sustain on purely literary grounds. It did not, to speak plainly, save the appearances, give an adequate account of the phenomena. Not incidentally, it was the interpretation most difficult to justify theologically. While the interpretations of Luther and Seripando have survived in one form or another down to the present day, the interpretation of Steinbach has fallen into well-deserved obscurity and is only resurrected by scholars as a historical curiosity. Luther and Seripando represented the wave of the future in Pauline studies, not only because they were the better theologians (I would be willing to defend that proposition without reservation), but also because they were the better literary critics.

3. I hope you will not misunderstand me when I say that the Bible was, in the fullest sense of the term, a sixteenth-century book. It influenced European attitudes toward war and peace, the structure of civil government and the family, the process of human growth and development, theories of child-rearing and education, as well as attitudes toward economic relations and policies of taxation. The Bible was appealed to by people who loved the church and who hated it; who hoped to reform society and who despaired of any fundamental progress in human relations; who were members of a cultured and highly literate elite, or who were illiterate and so were motivated to action by what they had been told by others. Sixteenth-century Europeans were comforted by the Bible in bereavement, used it to sanction marriages and contracts, bolstered their own wealth and position in society by a string of appropriate quotations, or were moved by the Bible to astonishing acts of self-renunciation and charity. The Bible was on the lips of religious martyrs—Roman Catholic, Protestant, and Anabaptist—and on the lips of their executioners. In the judgment of sixteenth-century Europeans, the Bible was worth both the dying and the killing for.

No other ancient authority—not Plato or Seneca or Cicero or Aristotle—could compete with the Bible in general importance or motivate more "sorts and conditions of men" into pursuing courses of action which, without the sanction of the Bible, they would have been reluctant to undertake. Indeed, no sixteenth-century author ever composed a book or poem or political treatise more influential in his own time than the Bible and, as you well know, some of the most important sixteenth-century plays, poems, political treatises, philosophical tracts, paintings, legal opinions, lists of *gravamina*, and private letters were intended—at least in part—to be extended comments on the biblical text. That was because the Bible was regarded by sixteenth-century Europeans as Scripture and not merely as an interesting and profitable book. A book which is regarded as Scripture is not, whatever one may think of it personally, just like any other book. It carries as divine revelation an *a priori* authority accorded by the community which acknowledges it to no other literary text.

In view of the fascination of the sixteenth century with the Bible, it is astonishing that so little attention has been paid by scholars to the history of biblical interpretation in the period from the death of Henry VIII of England to the accession of James VI of Scotland to the English throne. Progress may have been retarded by certain historians who can only understand the past if they attribute to unsympathetic and long-dead figures values which they themselves hold or which they can at least conceive of some of their contemporaries holding. Since the Bible is not important to them, much less Scripture, they dismiss it as a causative factor in sixteenth-century social, economic, and political life. Like nineteenth-century missionaries to the New Hebrides, they rush about replacing the grass skirts of the natives with suitable garments from the tailors of New England or New York. The past, however, remains stubbornly the past and our ancestors continue to believe, in spite of the shift in our values, exactly what they always believed.

There is one commandment, and one only, which historians, however frequently they may violate the other nine, must scrupulously observe or surrender their credentials, and that is, "Honor thy father and thy mother." That is to say, the past must be allowed to remain the past. It may not be remolded into our own image and likeness. If Philip of Hesse, Henry VIII of England, Christopher of Württemberg, Charles V of the House of Habsburg, and Christian II of Denmark regarded the Bible as authoritative Scripture, we had better find out what exactly that meant if we want to understand the political history of early modern Europe. The history of biblical interpretation is not incidental to European cultural history but central to it. The debates between Steinbach, Luther, and Seripando or More, Tyndale, Murner, and Henry VIII or Melanchthon, Eck, and Contarini are not a religious sideshow or pointless argy-bargy but reveal the aspirations, values, and failings of sixteenth-century Europe as nothing else can.

4. Which leads me to a final and concluding personal observation. We have slowly become aware in America that it is not possible to conduct medieval, renaissance, and reformation studies in isolation from each other and that the lines which divide the Mediaeval Academy from the Renaissance Society of America and the American Society for Reformation Research are dictated by the demands of the professional guilds to which we belong and not by the nature of the subject matter with which we are dealing. I am not as certain that we are fully aware that interdisciplinary approaches are not a luxury in medieval and renaissance studies but a necessity. Nowhere has this fact come home to me with more force than in my study of the history of biblical interpretation.

Literary theory, the history of philosophy and theology, cultural and social history, political theory, iconography, all intersect in the history of biblical interpretation. The lecture which I have given may very well be the last in the history of the Southeastern Institute of Medieval and Renaissance Studies. But even if the Tenth Institute proves to be the last, it will still have served an important function (as did the institutes before it) by bringing together scholars from diverse disciplines in a common task.

Occam could move with ease from logic to metaphysics to theology to political theory to epistemology. We who are expert in only one of the fields which Occam mastered find that we need the help of each other in order to understand our own special discipline correctly. The Southeastern Institute, by breaking down the artificial barriers which divide the disciplines from each other, has enabled each separate discipline to fulfill its own unique task more adequately. And for that, we are all grateful.

NOTES

1. This essay was written to mark the retirement of E. Gordon Rupp as Dixie Professor of Ecclesiastical History in the University of Cambridge and is offered to him in gratitude for his friendship, generosity, and unfailing kindnesses.

David C. Steinmetz

2. One can find a brief introduction to this dispute in my book *Reformers in the Wings* (Grand Rapids: Baker Book House, 1981), pp. 135–39.

3. On the importance of Abraham for Paul, see especially the stimulating essay by Ernst Käsemann, "The Faith of Abraham in Romans 4," in *Perspectives on Paul* (Philadelphia: Fortress Press, 1971), pp. 79–101.

4. The phrase is quoted by Heinrich Bullinger in his commentary on Romans. See H. Bullinger, *In Omnes Apostolicas Epistolas, Divi videlicet Pauli xiii. et vii. Canonicas, Commentarii* (Zurich), p. 47.

5. There are some exceptions to this rule as Maurice F. Wiles proves in his excellent book on the interpretation of Paul in the early church, *The Divine Apostle* (Cambridge: Cambridge University Press, 1967).

6. John B. Payne complains of this neglect in his fine essay, "Erasmus and Lefèvre d'Étaples as Interpreters of Paul," *Archiv für Reformationsgeschichte* 65 (1974): 54–83. See also the essays by Feld, Payne, Roussel, and Koch in *Histoire de l'exégèse au XVIᵉ siècle*, Olivier Fatio and Pierre Fraenkel, eds., *Etudes de philologie et d'histoire* 34 (Geneva: Librairie Droz, 1978), pp. 300–350.

7. Thomas de Vio, Cardinal Cajetan, *Epistolae Pauli et aliorum Apostolorum* (Paris, 1540).

8. Jacobus Sadoleto, Cardinal and Bishop of Carpentras, *Opera quae exstant omnia*, vol. IV (Verona, 1738).

9. Girolamo Seripando, Cardinal, *In Pauli Epistolas Commentaria* (Naples, 1601). [Hereafter cited as Seripando.]

10. For an introduction to Wendelin Steinbach and his biblical exegesis, see Helmut Feld, *Martin Luthers und Wendelin Steinbachs Vorlesungen über den Hebräerbrief* (Wiesbaden: Steiner, 1971) [Hereafter, *Hebräerbrief*]. Heiko Augustinus Oberman dissents from some of Feld's conclusions about Steinbach in his book, *Werden und Wertung der Reformation* (Tübingen: J. C. B. Mohr, 1977), pp. 118–40. As will become clear in what follows, I concur with Oberman in his dissent.

11. Helmut Feld, ed., *Wendelini Steinbach, Opera Exegetica Quae Supersunt Omnia*, vol. I (Wiesbaden: Steiner, 1976). [Hereafter cited as Steinbach.]

12. Zwingli's comments on Romans were published posthumously and may have undergone some revision by his editor. On Romans 4, see M. Schuler and J. Schulthess, eds., *Huldrici Zuinglii Opera*, vol. VI^2 (Zurich, 1833), pp. 88–91.

13. H. Bullinger, *Commentarii*, pp. 37–48.

14. Johannes Brenz, *Liber Commentariorum in Epistolam Pauli ad Romanos Primus, qui est de Fide* (Tübingen, 1588), pp. 550–68. This is printed as volume VII of the *Operum Reverendi et Clarissimi Theologi, D. Ioannis Brentii, Prepositi Stutgardiani*.

15. Philipp Melanchthon, *Commentarii in Epistolam Pauli ad Romanos*,

ed. Rolf Schäfer, *Melanchthons Werke in Auswahl*, vol. V (Gütersloher Verlagshaus Gerd Mohn, 1965), pp. 122–55.

16. A. Tholuck, ed., *Ioannis Calvini in Novi Testamenti Epistolas Commentarii*, vol. I (Berlin, 1834), pp. 45–58.

17. The standard work on Seripando is by Hubert Jedin, *Girolamo Seripando*, Cassiciacum II–III (Würzburg: Rita-Verlag, 1937).

18. Melanchthon, who was resident in Tübingen from 1512 to 1518 while pursuing his studies, called Steinbach an "adsiduus lector . . . sacrorum librorum, et Augustini." See Feld, *Hebräerbrief*, p. 9. Steinbach's marked copy of the Amerbach edition of Augustine has survived in the library of the University of Tübingen. See in this connection Oberman, *Werden und Wertung*, p. 120.

19. On the theology of Biel see H. A. Oberman, *The Harvest of Medieval Theology*, 3rd ed. (Durham, N.C.: The Labyrinth Press, 1983), pp. 131ff. For additional bibliography on this subject see my article "Late Medieval Nominalism and the *Clerk's Tale*," *The Chaucer Review* 12 (1977): 38–54, especially pp. 51–54.

20. Feld, *Hebräerbrief*, pp. 201–13; Oberman, *Werden und Wertung*, pp. 118–40.

21. Oberman, *Werden und Wertung*, p. 127.

22. Steinbach, III.17.136.1–7.

23. Steinbach, III.17.135.1–11.

24. Steinbach, V.30.262.24–28.

25. Feld, *Hebräerbrief*, pp. 208–9.

26. Steinbach, III.17.135.15–21.

27. Steinbach, III.18.142.14–143.1.

28. Steinbach, III.16.131.11–18.

29. Steinbach, III.17.134.20–25.

30. Steinbach, III.17.136.22–137.2.

31. Steinbach, V.30.264.5–8.

32. Steinbach, III.16.131.11–18; III.17.134.20–25; III.17.136.22–137.2.

33. Steinbach, III.17.134.12–17. See Oberman, *Werden und Wertung*, p. 127: "Das 'sola fide' wird damit nicht, wie bei Biel und in der Tradition üblich, zurückgewiesen, sondern als *modus loquendi* des Apostels—und Augustins—durchaus akzeptiert, jedoch nur für den christlichen Anfänger, der noch nicht voll im Bilde ist, dass der Glaube allein Gott keinesfalls genügt."

34. Steinbach, II.12.97.1–4; III.15.118.16–20; III.16.131.6–10; III.17.136.5–9; III.21.176.13–21. Cf. III.18.144.2–4; III.19.152.7–9.

35. Steinbach, III.16.129.26–130.6

36. Steinbach, III.19.152.7–9; III.15.118.16–20; III.15.119.1–15.

37. Steinbach, III.17.132.19–133.1; III.17.136.1–7.

38. Oberman, *Werden und Wertung*, p. 134.

39. *D. Martin Luthers Werke: Kritische Gesamtausgabe* (Weimar, 1883–), 1:224.7–8. [Hereafter *WA*.]

40. *WA* 56.423.19–20; 446.11–16; 446.31–32; 447.19–27.

41. *WA* 56.334.14–18; 371.2–10.

42. *WA* 4.168.1. Cf. *WA* 3.649.17–20.

43. *WA* 3.419.36–420.1.

44. *WA* 3.419.25–31.

45. *WA* 3.420.2–5.

46. *WA* 3.410.16–19.

47. *WA* 3.410.16–19.

48. *WA* 4.355.29–32.

49. *WA* 55^1.20.13–15; 55^2.106.16–19; 3.127.19–24; 3.311.35–36; 4.81.25–27; 4.337.10–12.

50. *WA* 3.548.2–5; 4.95.1–4; 4.356.9–13; 3.651.19–22; 4.83.3–9.

51. *WA* 57.236.1–7. I have cited the translation of James Atkinson, ed., *Luther: Early Theological Works, Library of Christian Classics* 16 (Philadelphia: Westminster Press, 1962), p. 213.

52. *WA* 55^2.123.19–22; 3.128.18–21; 4.40.14–15.

53. *WA* 3.199.16–18; 4.2.20; 4.13.13–27; 4.245.34–37.

54. *WA* 4.272.16–26; 3.180.24–26.

55. *WA* 3.410.16–19; 3.419.25–420.5; 3.649.17–20; 4.168.1.

56. *WA* 3.288.4–5; 3.284.21ff.; 3.292.27–32.

57. *WA* 3.291.9–21.

58. *WA* 3.289.31–35.

59. *WA* 4.375.16–20.

60. *WA* 4.262.2–7.

61. *WA* 3.288.6–32; 3.291.26–28; 55^2.24.6–12; 55^2.33.1–4.

62. *WA* 56.267.9–12.

63. *WA* 42.563. I have cited the translation of George Schick in *Luther's Works*, vol. III, J. Pelikan, ed. (St. Louis: Concordia Publishing House, 1961), pp. 20–21.

64. Seripando, p. 62.

65. Seripando, p. 65.

66. Seripando, p. 76.

67. Seripando, p. 65.

68. Seripando, pp. 448–49.

69. Seripando, pp. 72, 449–50.

70. Seripando, pp. 62–63.

71. Seripando, p. 62.

72. Seripando, p. 65.

73. Seripando, pp. 449–50.

74. Seripando, p. 450.

75. Seripando, pp. 64–65. Translation mine.

Appendix

Objectives

The Southeastern Institute of Medieval and Renaissance Studies was established for the advancement of scholarship and improvement of teaching. Through the Southeastern Institute, the resources of The University of North Carolina and Duke University—especially library holdings—were made available to scholars and teachers from throughout the nation. Participation was invited from those with scholarly interest in all areas of medieval and renaissance studies, including art, aesthetics, history, literature, music, paleography, philosophy, and religion.

The institute of 1979 consisted of five informal seminars, each concerned with a topic of interest to students of the medieval and renaissance periods. Each seminar was led by a Senior Fellow and had an enrollment of about six participants, designated Fellows. The typical seminar met twice weekly for one to two hours, but schedules were sufficiently flexible to permit arrangements adapted to the needs of the seminar. Each Fellow participated in one seminar and had ample free time to devote to his own research. It is emphasized that the seminars were not "courses" but informal meetings to encourage the exchange of ideas and to stimulate participants in their own research. Besides the seminars, the institute sponsored a public lecture by each of the Senior Fellows and held frequent coffee hours for those institute members who wished to attend.

Annually the institute alternated between the campuses of The University of North Carolina and Duke University. The tenth session, from June 18 to July 27, 1979, was held on the campus of The University of North Carolina at Chapel Hill.

Appendix

Seminars of the Tenth Session
June 18 to July 27, 1979

I. ITALIAN URBAN EXPERIENCE, 1200–1500.

SENIOR FELLOW: Dr. Gene Brucker, Professor of History, University of California, Berkeley. Guggenheim Fellow (1960–61); ACLS Fellow (1964–65); Fellow, Institute for Advanced Study, Princeton (1968–69); "Socio straniero," Deputazione di Storia Patria per la Toscana (1976); Fellow, Medieval Academy of America (1978).

AUTHOR: *Florentine Politics and Society, 1343–1378* (1962); *Renaissance Florence* (1969); editor, *The Society of Renaissance Florence* (1972); *The Civic World of Early Renaissance Florence* (1977); "The Medici in the Fourteenth Century," *Speculum* (1957); "Sorcery in Early Renaissance Florence," *Studies in the Renaissance* (1963); "The Ciompi Revolution," in N. Rubinstein, editor, *Florentine Studies* (1968); "Florence and Its University, 1348–1434," in T. Rabb and J. Seigel, editors, *Action and Conviction in Early Modern Europe* (1969); "The Florentine *Popolo Minuto* and Its Political Role, 1340–1450," in L. Martines, editor, *Violence and Civil Disorder in Italian Cities, 1200–1500* (1972).

DESCRIPTION: The seminar focused on significant issues in the recent historiography on urban experience in late medieval and renaissance Italy; e.g., the rise of the *signoria*; the fourteenth-century crisis; family structure; the Baron thesis; confraternities and urban piety; patronage.

II. LATIN CHRISTIAN TRADITION IN MEDIEVAL LITERATURE

SENIOR FELLOW: Dr. Robert E. Kaske, Avalon Foundation Professor in the Humanities, Cornell University. Guggenheim Fellow (1962–63 and 1977–78); Associate Member, Center for Advanced Study, University of Illinois (1962–63); Senior Fellow, American Council of Learned Societies (1971–72); Senior Fellow, Society for the Humanities, Cornell University (1972–73); Research Materials Grantee, National Endowment for the Humanities (1977–79); Original Member, Academy of Literary Studies (1972–); Chief Editor, *Traditio* (1975–); Member of Editorial and Advisory Committee, *A Manual of the Writings in Middle English* (1972–); Member of Editorial Board, *Variorum Chaucer* (1971–); Member of Editorial Board, *Chaucer Review* (1966–).

AUTHOR: "The Knight's Interruption of the *Monk's Tale*," *ELH: A Journal of English Literary History* 24 (1957); "*Sapientia et Fortitudo* as the Controlling Theme of *Beowulf*," *Studies in Philology* 55 (1958); "The Speech of 'Book' in *Piers Plowman*," *Anglia* 77 (1959); "An Aube in the *Reeve's Tale*," *ELH: A Journal of English Literary History* 26 (1959); "The Sigemund-Heremod and Hama-Hygelac Passages in *Beowulf*," *Publications of the Modern Language*

[116]

Association 74 (1959); "Two Cruxes in *Pearl*: 596 and 609–10," *Traditio* 15 (1959); "Patristic Exegesis in the Criticism of Medieval Literature: The Defense," *Critical Approaches to Medieval Literature: Selected Papers from the English Institute, 1958–1959* (1960); "Dante's 'DXV' and 'Veltro,'" *Traditio* 17 (1961); "The *Canticum Canticorum* in the *Miller's Tale*," *Studies in Philology* 59 (1962); "*Ex vi transicionis* and Its Passage in *Piers Plowman*," *Journal of English and Germanic Philology* 62 (1963); "Chaucer and Medieval Allegory," *ELH: A Journal of English Literary History* 30 (1963); "A Poem of the Cross in the Exeter Book: 'Riddle 60' and 'The Husband's Message,'" *Traditio* 23 (1967); "The *Eotenas* in *Beowulf*," *Old English Poetry: Fifteen Essays* (1967); "*Piers Plowman* and Local Iconography," *Journal of the Warburg and Courtauld Institutes* 31 (1968); "Some Newly Discovered Wall-Paintings at Madley, Herefordshire," *Traditio* 24 (1968); "Gawain's Green Chapel and the Cave at Wetton Mill," *Medieval Literature and Folklore Studies: Essays in Honor of Francis Lee Utley* (1970); "*Beowulf* and the Book of Enoch," *Speculum* 46 (1971); "Chaucer's Marriage Group," *Chaucer the Love Poet* (1973); "Holy Church's Speech and the Structure of *Piers Plowman*," *Chaucer and Middle English Studies in Honour of Rossell Hope Robbins* (1974); "Dante's *Purgatorio* XXXII and XXXIII: A Survey of Christian History," *University of Toronto Quarterly* 43 (1974); "The Conclusion of the Old English 'Descent into Hell,'" *παράδοσις: Studies in Memory of Edwin A. Quain* (1976).

DESCRIPTION: This seminar concentrated on the use of various large repositories of Christian tradition—for example the Vulgate Bible and its commentaries, encyclopedias, the liturgy, sermons and homilies, hymns and sequences, mythography, and the pictorial arts for the interpretation of medieval literature.

III. THE CICERONIAN TRADITION IN MEDIEVAL RHETORIC

SENIOR FELLOW: Dr. George Alexander Kennedy, Paddison Professor of Classics, The University of North Carolina at Chapel Hill. Kennedy Traveling Fellow (1954–55); Danforth Fellow (summer 1960); Fulbright Fellow (1964–65); Guggenheim Fellow (1965); National Endowment for the Humanities, Grantee (1968–69, 1970–71, 1972–73, 1974–77); Kenan Research Fellow (1971); American Council of Learned Societies, Grantee (1971).

AUTHOR: *The Art of Persuasion in Greece* (1963); *Quintilian* (1969); *The Art of Rhetoric in the Roman World* (1972); "Theophrastus and Stylistic Distinctions," *Harvard Studies in Classical Philology* 62 (1957); "The Ancient Dispute over Rhetoric in Homer," *American Journal of Philology* 78 (1957); "The Oratory of Andocides," *American Journal of Philology* 79 (1958); "Aristotle on the Period," *Harvard Studies in Classical Philology* 63 (1958); "The Earliest Rhetorical Handbooks," *American Journal of Philology* 80 (1959); "Isocrates' Encomium of Helen: A Panhellenic Document," *Transactions of the American Philological Association* 89 (1958); "Focusing of Arguments in Greek Deliberative Oratory," *Transactions of the American Philological Association* 90 (1959); "An Estimate of Quintilian," *American Journal of Philology* 83 (1962); "Non-Western Studies: A Challenge to the Classics," *Classical Journal* 58 (1963); "Two Problems in the Historical Study of Rhetoric," *Pennsylvania Speech Annual* 21 (1964); "Speech Education in Greece," *Western Speech* 31 (1967); "Crassus, Cicero, and Caplan," *Addresses Delivered at the Meeting Honoring Professor Harry Caplan* (1967); "The Oratorical Career of Demosthenes," in *Demosthenes On the Crown*, edited by J. J. Murphy (1967); "Antony's Speech at Caesar's Funeral," *Quarterly Journal of Speech* 54 (1968); "The Rhetoric of Advocacy in Greece and Rome," *American Journal of Philology* 89 (1968); "The Shadow of Isocrates," *Colorado Journal of Educational Research* 2 (1972); "The Present State of the Study of Ancient Rhetoric," *Classical Philology* 70 (1975); "Classical Influences on *The Federalist*," *Classical Traditions in Early America*, edited by J. W. Eadie, Ann Arbor: Center for Coordination of Ancient and Modern Studies (1976); "A Southerner in the Peloponnesian War," *Southern Humanities Review* (Special issue: The Classical Tradition in the South, 1977); "Encolpius and Agamemnon in Petronius," *American Journal of Philology* 99 (1978); "Classical and Christian Source Criticism," in *The Relationship Among the Gospels*, edited by William O. Walker, Jr. (1978).

DESCRIPTION: After brief consideration of the composition and contents of the Ciceronian rhetorical corpus (including *Rhetorica ad Herennium* and *Topica*), the seminar investigated how Ciceronian theory was understood, used, or adapted by a variety of medieval teachers, writers, or speakers from St. Augustine to the School of Chartres.

IV. ENGLISH PASTORAL POETRY, SPENSER TO MILTON

SENIOR FELLOW: Dr. Louis Lohr Martz, Sterling Professor of English, Yale University; Director, Beinecke Rare Book and Manuscript Library, Yale University (1972–78); Guggenheim Fellow (1948–49); Rockefeller Foundation, Grantee (1966–67); National Endowment for the Humanities, Fellow (1977–78); Christian Gauss Prize, Phi Beta Kappa (1955); Chairman, Yale Edition, *The Complete Works of St. Thomas More*; Fellow, American Academy of Arts and Sciences.

AUTHOR: *The Poetry of Meditation: A Study in English Religious Literature of the Seventeenth Century* (1954); *The Paradise Within: Studies in Vaughan, Traherne, and Milton* (1964); *The Poem of the Mind: Essays on Poetry, English and American* (1966); *The Wit of Love: Donne, Carew, Crashaw, Marvell* (1969); *Thomas More's Prayer Book: A Facsimile Reproduction of the Annotated Pages* (1969); "Hero and Leander" by Christopher Marlowe (1972); "A Dialogue of Comfort Against Tribulation" by Thomas More (1976); "The Rising Poet, 1645," in *The Lyric and Dramatic Milton*, edited by Joseph H. Summers, English Institute Essays (1965); "Chorus and Character in *Samson Agonis-*

tes," Milton Studies 1 (1969); *"Paradise Lost:* Princes of Exile," ELH 36 (1969); *"Paradise Lost:* The Power of Choice," *Ventures* 10 (1970); *"Paradise Lost:* The Realms of Light," *English Literary Renaissance* 1 (1971); "Camoens and Milton," *Ocidente* (Lisbon) 35 (1972); "Who is Lycidas?" *Yale French Studies* 47 (1972); "The Music of *Comus,"* in *Illustrious Evidence: Approaches to English Literature of the Early Seventeenth Century,* edited by Earl Miner (1975); *"Paradise Lost:* The Solitary Way," in *The Author in His Work,* edited by L. Martz and A. Williams (1978); "The *Amoretti:* Most Goodly Tempera-ture," in *Form and Convention in the Poetry of Edmund Spenser,* edited by William Nelson, English Institute Essays (1961); "The Design of More's *Dialogue of Comfort," Moreana* 15 (1967); "The Action of the Self: Devotional Poetry in the Seventeenth Century," in *Stratford-Upon-Avon Studies, II: Metaphysical Poetry,* edited by Malcolm Bradbury and D. J. Palmer (1970); "Donne's *Anniversaries* Revisited," in *That Subtile Wreath: Lectures Presented at the Quatercentenary Celebration of the Birth of John Donne* (1972); "Thomas More: The Tower Works," in *St. Thomas More: Action and Contemplation,* edited by R. S. Sylvester (1972); "Thomas More: The Sacramental Life," *Thought* 52 (1977).

DESCRIPTION: This seminar explored the pastoral tradition of Theocritus and Vergil as represented and extended in Spenser's *Shepheardes Calender* and portions of the *Faerie Queene;* Shakespeare's *Winter's Tale;* Milton's *Co-mus, Lycidas,* and portions of *Paradise Lost;* and the pastoral poems of Marvell and Herrick.

V. THE INTERPRETATION OF THE BIBLE IN THE SIXTEENTH CENTURY

SENIOR FELLOW: Dr. David C. Steinmetz, Professor of Church History, Duke University. American Association of Theological Schools Faculty Fellow (1970–71); Guggenheim Fellow (1977–78); Research Grants, Ameri-can Council of Learned Societies (1973), the Andrew W. Mellon Founda-tion (1977–78), and the Arthur Vining Davis Foundation (1977–78); Edito-rial Board, *Duke University Monographs in Medieval and Renaissance Studies* (1972–); Board of Consultants, *The Harvard Theological Review* (1975–); Board of Editors, *Archiv für Reformationsgeschichte* (1977–); Council, the American Society of Church History (1974–76), and the American Society for Reformation Research (1977–79).

AUTHOR: *Misericordia Dei: The Theology of Johannes von Staupitz in its Late Medieval Setting* (1968); *Reformers in the Wings* (1971); "The Nature of Ordi-nation in the Light of Tradition," *Lancaster Theological Seminary Bulletin* 3 (1969); "Scholasticism and Radical Reform: Nominalist Motifs in the The-ology of Balthasar Hubmaier," *The Mennonite Quarterly Review* 45 (1971); *"Libertas Christiana:* Studies in the Theology of John Pupper of Goch (d. 1475)," *The Harvard Theological Review* 55 (1972); "Luther and the Late Me-dieval Augustinians: Another Look," *The Concordia Theological Monthly* 44

(1973); "Protestantism" and other entries, *The New International Dictionary of the Christian Church* (1975); "Mary Reconsidered," *Christianity Today* 20 (1975); "Asbury's Doctrine of Ministry," *The Duke Divinity School Review* 40 (1975); "The Necessity of History," *Theology Today* 33 (1976); "Theological Reflections on the Reformation and the Status of Women," *The Duke Divinity School Review* 41 (1976); "Luther ausserhalb des Luthertums: Reformierte Sicht," *Concilium* 12 (1976); "Theology and Exegesis: Ten Theses," in *Actes du Colloque de l'exégèse biblique au XVIe siècle* (1976); "Reformation and Conversion," *Theology Today* 35 (1978); "Late Medieval Nominalism and the *Clerk's Tale*," *The Chaucer Review* 13 (1979); "Hermeneutic and Old Testament Interpretation in Staupitz and the Young Martin Luther," *Archiv für Reformationsgeschichte* 70 (1979); "The Baptism of John and the Baptism of Jesus in Huldrych Zwingli, Balthasar Hubmaier and Late Medieval Theology," in *Festschrift for George H. Williams* (1979).

DESCRIPTION: The theory and practice of biblical interpretation during the Reformation period against the background of patristic and medieval exegesis.

Fellows of the Southeastern Institute of Medieval and Renaissance Studies, 1979

Seminar 1
Sarah Rubin Blanshei (University of Tennessee)
Melissa Bullard (University of North Carolina at Chapel Hill)
George Lawrence Gorse (Dumbarton Oaks)
Edward Wallace Muir, Jr. (Syracuse University)
Brenda Isabel Preyer (University of Texas at Austin)
Anne Jacobson Schutte (Lawrence University)

Seminar 2
Ira R. Adams (Sam Houston State University)
Alan Kelsey Brown (Ohio State University at Columbus)
Dennis John Costa (Boston University)
Thomas John Andrew Heffernan (University of Tennessee)
John DeWitt Niles (University of California at Berkeley)
Judith Davis Shaw (University of Georgia at Athens)

Seminar 3
Martin Camargo (University of Missouri at Columbia)
Michael Charles Leff (University of California at Davis)
Caroline Ruth Locher (Pacific University)
James Michael May (St. Olaf College)

Seminar 4
Andrew Ettin (Wake Forest University)
David G. Hale (State University of New York at Brockport)
Frederick P. Kiefer (University of Arizona)
Alice Cornelia Loftin (VPI and SU)
Edward Lee Piepho (Sweet Briar College)
David A. Richardson (Cleveland State University)

Seminar 5

Cherie Ann Haeger (Gannon College)
Richard Leigh Harrison, Jr. (Eureka College)
Thomas Eugene Helm (Western Illinois University)
Edward Craney Jacobs (Louisiana Tech University)
Anne Mary O'Donnell, S.N.D. (Catholic University of America)
Louis John Reith (East Carolina University)